Additional praise for *Corkscrewed*:

"If you think you would enjoy having a conversation with a passionate French wine craftsman, dive into Robert Camuto's delicious new book. I spend a good part of my life underground in France, and everything Camuto relates of his adventures rings true. And to those of you tiring of the varietal bandwagon, here's an escape route." —Kermit Lynch, wine importer and author of *Adventures on the Wine Route: A Wine Buyer's Tour of France*

"[Camuto's] enthusiasm for underdog grapes, regions and winemakers makes him a pleasant guide along the back roads of France." —Thomas Matthews, *Wine Spectator*

"If you saw and liked the film *Mondovino*, get this book. Like a collection of love letters to wine, each chapter showcases a winemaker who has carved out a niche for himself amid the encroaching corporate tide, sprawl, or commercialization. In a world of oak chips and cost-benefit analysis, these are the winemakers who must endure, even in beloved France." —Maggie Savarino Dutton, *Seattle Weekly*

"Mr. Camuto's writing is precise, entertaining and compelling enough that it should appeal to audiences beyond the normally narrow scope reached by wine books. It reads very much like a collection of short stories that come together to form what is essentially a non-fiction novel. It travels a road that I'd very much like to follow. The individual stories alone are very much worth the price of admission. The fact that they come together to form a much greater whole makes *Corkscrewed* a rare gem in the field of wine literature and a highly recommended read." —David McDuff, *McDuff's Food and Wine Trail*

"[Camuto] is a stylish writer with a gift for describing the way his subjects look and think, and express themselves in words and wine. He explains each winemaker's approach and results, also adding a bit of insight about intra-French competition and the export market in the French wine industry today." —Claire Walter, Culinarycolorado.com

"Deliciously descriptive, Camuto is informative without being too technical, a serious observer yet humorously light-hearted at times." —Julia Lauer-Cheenne, *Lincoln (NE) Journal Star*

BISON
BOOKS

WITHDRAWN

AT TABLE   UNIVERSITY OF NEBRASKA PRESS : LINCOLN AND LONDON

ROBERT V. CAMUTO

With a new preface by the author

CORKSCREWED

Adventures

in the

New French

Wine Country

© 2008 by Robert V. Camuto
Preface © 2010 by the Board of Regents of
the University of Nebraska
All rights reserved
Manufactured in the United States of America
⊛
First Nebraska paperback printing: 2010

All photographs courtesy of the author.

Library of Congress
Cataloging-in-Publication Data

Camuto, Robert V.
Corkscrewed : adventures in the new French
wine country / Robert V. Camuto.
p. cm. — (At table)
ISBN 978-0-8032-7635-2 (cloth : alk. paper)
ISBN 978-0-8032-2978-5 (paper : alk. paper)
1. Wine and wine making—France—Anecdotes.
2. Wineries—France—Anecdotes. I. Title.
II. Title: Adventures in the new French wine
country. III. Series: At table series.
TP553.C256 2008
641.2'20944—dc22   2008024069

Designed and set in Sabon
by Ashley Muehlbauer.

DURING THOSE STRANGE DAYS around the beginning of the Iraq War, I wondered if anyone in America would ever read a book about French wine again. As French water, French cheese, French perfume, and even "French fries" were boycotted in a swell of patriotic righteousness and French wine was being poured into gutters before television cameras, I had doubts.

When *Corkscrewed* was published in November 2008, the darkest days of Francophobia were over, and fries could be called "French" again. Only, a new crisis had gripped the United States and the world in the form of a financial meltdown. Again, I wondered, in such grave times how much interest would there be in new generations of French *vignerons* reshaping the wine world?

As it turned out—lots.

What I discovered on my subsequent trips to my homeland amazed me. Audiences—much younger than the classic middle-aged, wine-swirling public—were hungry to learn about *real* food and wine. A generation that grew up with chicken nuggets and thirty-two-ounce Cokes was searching for basic values tied to the land in a world that seemed to have spun off its axis with mindless pay-later consumerism. Much of this credit for the raising of consciousness goes to Michael Pollan, whose book *The Omnivore's Dilemma* eloquently critiques the disconnect of the industrial food chain and has created a hunger—and thirst—for alternatives.

In some ways, the financial crisis has been perversely good for wine—deflating its greedy exploitation as a luxury product and snob accessory at the top of the market and fostering a return to both *values* and *value*. It was natural that France lead the renaissance of real wines grown with nonchemical farming and made with simple, low-tech processes. For nowhere else has the number of winemakers, the diversity of *terroirs* and traditions, and a comparable population of ungovernable rural philosophers.

As "authentic" or "natural" wines have blossomed around the world, so has consumer choice. More people now *get* the French idea of *terroir*, and they understand that great wines shouldn't all taste alike. If there is a small price to pay for this, it is in the impulse of us Americans to take any trend, label it to death, and try to turn it into a lifestyle brand. Wine snobbism persists—though now it often has a new, antiestablishment face.

All snobbery debases wine. As much as wine should be a natural product, it should be *a natural part of life*: food for body and soul. The wine world should be about freedom, discovery, humility, and humanity. In *Corkscrewed* I worked to show how these realms come together in France's vineyards. I have been rewarded by many e-mails and notes from readers who had little interest in "wine books" but grew fascinated with the people and places in *Corkscrewed* and their relevance in these times.

I invite you all to join the continuing journey at www.corkscrewed .info.

To Dantino, who made '94 the finest vintage.
And to winemakers everywhere who resist
doing *n'importe quoi.*

Quickly bring me a beaker of wine, so that I may whet my mind and say something clever.
—ARISTOPHANES

We are all mortal until the first kiss and the second glass of wine. —EDUARDO GALEANO, *The Book of Embraces*

CONTENTS

Illustrations

Acknowledgments

Exploring wine should be done in good company, which I have not lacked.

Since we moved to France in 2001, my wife, Gilda, and son, Dantino, have been patient and indulgent travel companions, supportive of my peripatetic research.

Fellow wine musketeers who've participated in this journey include Daniel Schmitt, Ken and Joyce Mc-Neill, Philippe Boué, the Le Toumelin family, Sally Vetter, Jacques Metais, and the Union of Sommeliers de Provence–Nice–Cote d'Azur. And, of course, Uncle Jacques Battude.

I am appreciative of all the winemakers featured in this book, especially François des Ligneris and Arnaud Daudier de Cassini in Saint-Émilion and Claude and Olivia Martin in Les Mayons—who generously gave of themselves beyond my expectations.

The publication of *Corkscrewed* meant an opportunity to forge some new relationships with wine lovers, merchants, wine bars, and independent booksellers on two continents who are too numerous to list here. I am particularly grateful to Art Nelson for hosting me in Seattle and to the wine importers who shared wines from the book, including Kermit Lynch Wine Merchant, Jenny & Francois Selections / World Wide Wine, Charles Neal Selections, Millesime, and Martin Scott Wines.

C
o
r
k
s
c
r
e
w
e
d

As the Corkscrew Turns

IT WAS A PERFECT DAY to lose faith in wine. By midmorning on June 21, 2005, the heat and humidity were conspiring to make it another in a series of stifling hot days in Bordeaux. I'd set out from Saint-Émilion in my tiny Citroën rental car—windows rolled down to make up for the lack of air conditioning—en route to Vinexpo, the world's largest wine convention held once every two years in the sprawling convention site north of the city.

As I inched along in traffic across the bridge on the Gironde River, I was thinking about the schizophrenic state of the French wine industry, which—if you believed the French—was in a state of inescapable crisis. Winemakers were rioting in Languedoc, furious over global competition and circumstances beyond their control. French people were drinking less, having ceded to the Italians their place as the world's biggest wine drinkers. While Americans were learning from study after study about the positive effects of red wine, French government health campaigns were targeting their country-men's overconsumption. (To show just how serious the Republic was about cutting down on drinking and driving, gendarmes were going after the once-sacrosanct Sunday lunch crowd by staking out traffic circles across the countryside.) French wine by the tanker was going unsold, and prices of run-of-the mill wines were collapsing as the once-untouchable French wine industry appeared to be drowning in foreign wines from places like Chile, where French winemakers had taken their savoir faire. Even French actor, winemaker, and bon vivant Gérard Depardieu was quoted in news articles saying he hadn't had a drink in six months! As for the French intellectuals,

1. A vineyard near Wolxheim, Alsace

what could they do but write essays proclaiming the end of France's wine glory?

Yet, in a seemingly cruel and simultaneous twist, the forces of globalization were inflating prices of the grandest of Bordeaux's *grand crus*, wines that were already out of the reach of most mortals. Bottles of most anything French and expensive were being snapped up as status symbols—like luxury watches—by freshly minted millionaires in Russia and China who, it was said, drank Petrus with Coca-Cola.

Just the day before, I'd lunched at Saint-Émilion's legendary

Château Cheval Blanc, which is owned by a pair of regulars on the *World's Richest* list: Bernard Arnault, the French founder and chief of Louis Vuitton Möet Hennessy, the world's leading luxury brand conglomerate, and Belgian industrialist Baron Frère. The aim of the lunch was to promote Cheval Blanc's adopted and renamed Argentinean family member, Cheval des Andes, which commanded about $70 a bottle (cheap by Cheval Blanc standards).

I was seated at this lunch next to a fellow American—a wine writer who told me he also happened to run a wine fund on the side.

"A wine what?"

A "wine fund," he explained, bought wine futures with investors' money for speculation. "It represents," he said apologetically, "the dark side of wine."

From the champagne and *amuses-bouches* delivered by white-jacketed roaming servers on the terrace, through the gazpacho and grilled steak accompanied by several vintages of the bold Argentinean red in the garden dining room, to the languorous finale of cigars and cognac on outdoor sofas under the shade of canvas umbrellas, one had to be impressed. Cheval Blanc's soft-spoken managing director and legendary winemaker Pierre Lurton quietly made the rounds, his mouth stuck in a kind of permanent smile that betrayed the possibility that schmoozing might not be his thing. Then the guests departed in a stampede of Mercedeses that left a trail of dust along the picturesque plateau of vines.

After arriving at Vinexpo, it didn't take long for me to feel as though I'd landed in another Oz. Three modern convention halls and acres upon acres of thousands of displays featured wine from just about anywhere grapes grow: from Syria to Lebanon to Israel to China. Prestige French, Spanish, and Italian wine groups showed off with opulent installations resembling five-star hotel lobbies complete with marble floors, plush wool carpets, and tasting bars and lounges equipped with furniture you could sink into and disappear. Amid it all were cries of "Mon cher ami!"—the universal business mating call of a population of mostly men in dark business suits, pronounced with English, Japanese, and German accents or the Bordeaux salesman's overly nasal French.

I made my way to the Bordeaux-Aquitane installation, where I learned that at 10 a.m. Serena Sutcliffe, the British-born former head of Sotheby's international wine department and one of the most respected tasters in the wine world, would be leading a "Balade en Bordeaux" (a stroll through Bordeaux) tasting while holding forth to a live audience. Nearly six feet tall and about sixty years old, with fairylike white hair pulled back in a ponytail and endowed with a long, formidable schnoz, Sutcliffe cut an impressive figure—accentuated by her above-the-knee skirt and chic pink T-shirt.

A glass of wine in one hand, a cordless microphone in the other, and never far from a spittoon, Sutcliffe began her discourse with white wines, speaking to about twenty or so people who followed her around with wineglasses. The first wine, from the Bordeaux region Entre-deux-Mers, she noted as "tropicale" in its fruitiness; the second, from Bordeaux Superior, was the product of drought and small production: a "vraie manque d'eau" (drought) that led to a "petite recolte" (small harvest). Above the din, Sutcliffe spoke about climate and grapes, delivering her impressions in deliberate, fluent, British-accented French. Moving on to the reds and a 2002 from Graves, she pronounced its nose "typ-iqu-e-ment Pessac" (typical of Pessac) with scents of "tabac Havane" (Havana tobacco).

I looked around: the crowd seemed to be only half-listening. I overheard some discussion among organizers about a problem with the acoustics. Sutcliffe's mic was turned up.

It wasn't anything Sutcliffe had said that made the scene so disturbingly odd. Maybe it was the imposing microphone she was holding, or the way she seemed to be speaking to a point somewhere over our heads. Or maybe it was the idea of an "expert" commentator holding forth on a subject as personal as wine. Almost every aspect of life has become mediated—saturated by experts who provide instant analysis and emotion and tell the rest of us what to think and feel. Had wine become no different? Indeed, here was a "celebrity" wine taster performing a sort of electronic circus ritual: life imitates television. Real or CNN?

I fled to an exhibition room that was holding one of the most popular programs of the week, presented by the Union des Grands

Crus de Bordeaux. More than one hundred wines from the yet-to-be-released 2004 vintage were offered by many of Bordeaux's prestigious châteaux. But with each mouthful I took—from Pauillac to Saint-Émilion, from Pomerol to Saint Estephe—the wines seemed to taste more and more alike: young and rude with raging tannins that made my tongue and the inside of my mouth feel as though they'd been freshly lacquered. The room was full of buyers, sellers, marketers, sommeliers, and consultants (along with my "dark side of wine" acquaintance) who dutifully sniffed, slurped, swished, and spit out scores of Bordeaux's finest reds and whites, then huddled in small groups to handicap the stuff with the dour calculation of stockbrokers.

Happily, there is another, brighter side to wine: Outside the velvet-rope corral of the wine elite and the factory walls of multinational wineries, we are living in a golden age for wine diversity, quality, and discovery. It's a movement led by small producers the world over, though their wines are not always easy to find. (Little guys don't have the same access to the distribution chain and your supermarket shelves.)

And what is true for wine in general goes double for France, still the world's largest producer of fine wines. No other place on earth has the astounding diversity of wine regions, microclimates, and independent producers. France is almost one-third larger than the state of California but has about four times the acreage of vineyards. Some 78,000 winegrowers—nearly eighteen times more than in California—operate in France's 472 wine appellations (and that accounts for only about half of France's wine production; the other half of French wine is made outside the appellations). New generations of French winemakers are producing smaller quantities of better wines, reflective of their regions and bearing little resemblance to the bulk cooperative wines made by their parents. The quality revolution in France is transforming not only the wine but also the wine-producing countryside. With increasing numbers and vehemence, winemakers are rejecting herbicides, pesticides, chemical fertilizers, and winery tricks to produce wines from grape varieties that were considered obsolete a generation ago. This is good for the wine, good for the environment, and good for the intrepid wine lover.

I was born, by the way, a long way from any vineyards, in New York City. My first memory of wine was when I was four or five years old in my grandparents' apartment. My Neapolitan grandfather gave me the job of opening his bottles of pungent, 1960s-era Chianti that mingled with the aromas of my grandmother's meaty pasta sauce that had cooked in wine all day long. My grandfather, who died when I was six, was an unflappable, generous man who came to America as a youth, made money, lost it in '29, and restarted life with a small grocery store on lower First Avenue. In the basement of his store he made wine.

For most of my adult life, I thought of wine as a drink—a drink more satisfying, intriguing, and heady than beer, but still a drink. Over the years of married life in Texas—where I worked as a journalist and later as founder and publisher of an alternative newspaper—I appreciated a range of wines as wide as the stocks of local wine sellers. But the small wine rack in our kitchen pantry was usually empty, the result of our inability to buy wine faster than we consumed it.

Everything I'd ever thought about wine began to change in the summer of 2001 after I sold the newspaper and house in Texas and moved to France with my wife, Gilda—who was born in Nice but was reared in California—and our son, Alexander Dante ("Dantino"), who had spent his first seven years in Dallas–Fort Worth, Texas.

That year we bought and began making plans to renovate our new home: an eighteenth-century olive oil mill in the countryside outside of Grasse. There were no vineyards in our village—just the small plots of vines that peasants had used not long ago to make their own personal stocks. But the one feature of the place that sold me was the series of old stone-and-falling-mortar vaulted rooms under the mill. This cool, damp cave was filled with mold and cobwebs, and lit by dim bulbs hanging from frayed wires. It also happened to be filled with thousands of bottles of French wine—a real cellar. At a moment when negotiations were completed and all that remained was the actual exchange of signatures, money, and keys at the notary's office, the old proprietor of the place—a wily Frenchman I shall call Monsieur A.—took me down to the cellar.

A man of about sixty who had a bad leg and walked with a cane, Monsieur A. was eager to sell because of his estrangement and imminent divorce from the much younger Madame A. Monsieur A., dressed in a pressed shirt and blazer, put his free hand on my shoulder as we walked among decades-old bottles from Burgundian villages and Bordeaux estates: "What will you have?" Monsieur A. purred into my ear as he invited me to pick a case of twelve bottles out of the cellar to keep. This was, I suspected, not so much a gesture of generosity as it was a way of cinching the deal—and keeping me from backing out.

In fact, I didn't know quite where to start, and selected the wines almost blindly. I had a lot to learn about wine and France, a fact that was underscored as we left the cellar: as we stepped into the sunlight, Monsieur A. cooed in French-accented English over my shoulder, "And if you ever need anything from the mayor [of our new village], he loves his *grands crus*." Since that winter day, I've crisscrossed France many times, visiting, drinking, and even working in the vineyards. I no longer think of wine as a drink.

One of my earliest surprises living in France was discovering just how present wine is at every level of society. I remember seeing in American market surveys that wine is a product generally associated with class and education. In France I noticed that wine wasn't found just at restaurants, bistros, and cafés, but at truck stops, school picnics, and parent-teacher outings. As a tourist I had associated everything in France with "quaint." I was stunned to learn that France has hypermarkets that make Wal-Mart look like a convenience store and where salespeople roam the aisles on roller skates. These stores had wine departments unlike anything I could have imagined: on their own they could be considered wine superstores, with reds, whites, rosés, *crémants* (sparkling wines), sweet wines, and fortified wines, arranged by region from most corners of France. These departments were presided over by male and female sommeliers in burgundy-colored aprons who offered tastes of featured wines of the week. When they offered their wine sales in fall, I watched people fill their grocery carts to the brim with cases of the stuff. Everywhere I turned there seemed to be acres of wine at prices sometimes cheaper than mineral water.

Sometimes wine came from unexpected places. Even the city of Nice had a miniscule appellation of Bellet, which my wife and I explored going door to door and knocking until someone would sell us a few bottles. We tasted a different wine almost every night—usually indiscriminately and often irrespective of what we were eating. Pauillac with pizza? Echézeaux with barbeque? *Pourquoi pas?*

Over time, that changed as I discovered the pleasure—second nature in France with its myriad cuisines—of pairing wine with foods. I was introduced to the sommeliers' association of our region, Nice–Provence–Côte d'Azur–Corsica (although Corsica, true to form, later seceded), and I was invited to join. This association was full of professional sommeliers, wine enthusiasts, and students learning from the seasoned professionals who could wax eloquent about the wine's *robe*, or appearance, its nose, its attack, its ending, and yes, of course, its taste. Here I learned a new vocabulary of wine (in French), but—more important—as I listened to these sommeliers, I noticed that their flowery, often dubious, oratories always ended with mouth-watering food pairings, from wild hare in olives to duck flanks in sage, from Roquefort cheese to chocolate.

As I traveled through France, I made a point of visiting vineyards. Seeing and tasting wine in the areas where it was grown with the foods of the region taught me two things. First, I learned that wine is not so much a drink to pair with foods as *it is a food*. Wine is an important food group that has evolved with regional palates. The long, acid-polished wines of Burgundy, for example, fit hand-in-glove with Burgundian preparations of escargots, terrines of parsleyed hams, Bresse chicken and Charolais beef cooked in wine, and sauces of butter, cream, and mustards. The full-fruit wines of Provence are made for the simple olive oil and Italian-influenced dishes like stuffed zucchini flowers, pasta *pistou*, or octopus salad. *Vin jaune* from the mountains of the Jura (a slow-fermented and long-aged "yellow" wine that can be kept for a century or more) goes perfectly with a bird drowned in that same wine or with a hot, oozing round of stinky Mont d'Or cheese. At Christmastime those French supermarkets moved foie gras by the ton along with naturally sweet wines from Sauternes, Monbazillac, the Loire Valley, or Alsace.

The second thing I experienced was *terroir*. It was one thing to understand terroir—the concept that soil, climate, winds, exposition, and other seemingly cosmic factors affect wines. It's another thing to *witness* it. I tasted syrah in wines in the Mediterranean part of the Rhône Valley in the south of France that were stout and aromatically explosive. Then I experienced the same grape variety a couple of hours due north in the cool, temperate climate of Côte Rôtie, where the wine turned out lean and elegant. I saw that a vineyard on one hillside could produce a completely different wine from the vineyard on the plain or on a hill across the road. Everywhere I went, I saw that the vineyards producing the most interesting and complex wines had been exploited since antiquity. The Romans, it seemed, knew their wine and marked the best real estate. *Veni, vidi, vici* translated to "location, location, location."

Terroir is not new to France: the idea has been cultivated, advanced, and codified here as nowhere else. It is fairly new to us Americans, who tend to think more in broad black-and-white terms. To see the difference, you need look no further than wine labels. In California, Australia, and most of the New World, wines are classified foremost by what Americans see as the best way to determine *what they are*—grape variety. In France (with the notable exception of Germanic Alsace), where wines are often blends of several grapes depending on the harvest, wines are first classified by *where they are from*—terroir. In California, for example, pinot noir is called pinot noir. In Burgundy, where pinot noir is really the only red wine grape, the subregions and villages—with names such as Pernand Vergelesses, Gevrey-Chambertin, and Nuits-Saint-George—determine what the wine truly is.

In the New World we also tend to place more faith in better living through science and modern know-how. I've heard wine merchants in the states try to use "technology" as a selling point for wine, as though they were selling the latest electronic gadget. Their point is that with modern techniques you could make a great wine almost *anywhere*. Technological winemaking, as developed by industrial winemakers in places like California and Australia and practiced to an extent now in the Old World, means drought-free summers because of irrigation; it means you don't have to wait for vines to mature fifteen years or more to develop "character"; it means adding acid to wine in hot years to lighten it; using flavor-inducing yeasts (or in some cases even essences) to seduce the nose with banana, kiwi, or ripe raspberry; dropping in wood chips to give it a toasty, vanilla flavor. Technology means no more "bad" years for wine, yet it also means no great or surprising vintages—just a perpetual assembly line of high-octane wines that tend to taste alike.

Wine is, naturally, a product of three elements: terroir, grape-vines, and the winemaker. I am not against technology; I just think it should be used for other things like curing disease or making cleaner cars. My friend Arnaud Daudier de Cassini—a gentleman and microwine producer in Saint-Émilion—once philosophized in a conversation of wine-drinking men: "I could sleep with *putes* (whores), but even if they were more beautiful than my wife, what would be the point? How would I ever know what was real? What I have with my wife I know is real." And so, in my humble opinion, it should be with wine.

In France's vineyards there is now a backlash to the idea, which took hold after World War II, that to be "modern" meant to use the full range of herbicides, pesticides, and chemical fertilizers and treatments. France's terroirs are beginning to breathe again, a fact that is signified by the weeds and natural grasses now being allowed to sprout between vine rows and the sheep that are put to pasture in vineyards in winter.

At minimum, responsible winemakers use a "reasoned agriculture," limiting chemicals except in extreme cases. Many use organic agriculture with no synthetic products in the vineyard. More and more are turning to the holistic approach of biodynamics, which uses natural remedies and plants, timed to the cycles of the moon to return life to vineyard soils.

There is no one formula for great winemaking. One thing that great wines have in common is a winemaker *who is in the vineyard and who is close to his or her vines*. If I meet a winemaker in the fall around the time of the grape harvest, and he has a good manicure and unstained hands, I probably won't buy his wine.

No other agricultural product touches us like wine. Humans shape wine and give it its soul, but wine also shapes the people who make it, often on a level that is spiritually profound. In the vineyards of France, I have met scores of people with uncommon grace, humility, good sense, and wisdom. It is among these small, passionate winegrowers that I feel something very close to a state of *home*.

Among the small winemakers of France, I find much the same spirit of generosity and courage as in my grandfather's generation of Europeans. Today's *paysans* are well educated in modern schools, yet they are—to a degree that's rare in today's world—fully immersed in life. It's a life that combines hard work with the realm of sensuous gustatory pleasure; the marketplace with patrimony; economics with philosophy. And it's all tied to the forces of nature and its whims. The adventures in this book are intended to provide a glimpse into that world.

You can hardly discuss wine anymore without broaching the subject of Robert Parker, the American wine critic, publisher of the *Wine Advocate*, and one of the most feared and revered people in the world of wine. A lot of baggage has been laid at Parker's feet—some of it unjustified. At a dinner one evening at an inn in the Ardèche, I was seated next to a wine lover from Strasbourg. We discussed the French government's decision to allow wood chips in wine vats for the first time, and he said, "It's all because of Monsieur Parker." This was ridiculous, I replied. While Monsieur Parker may be responsible for the preponderance of what the French call a "Parkerized" wine style of big, blockbuster, and even woody wines, the man is an avowed foe of shortcuts. The biggest problem with Parker's one-man 100-point system in particular, and similar grading scales in general, is that they contribute to an illusory and narrow star system, on which the Dark Lords of Wine from Bordeaux to Napa to Tuscany have been expert in capitalizing.

Fortunately for the intrepid among us, there are thousands of French wines, many of which fall under the radar of the arbiters of good taste, made by serious vintners with a greater connection to wine than the corporate investors or insurance companies that now own many a Bordeaux château.

The new French wine country of small regional producers is not a world that all of France embraces. *La Republique*, after all, has one foot in its patrimony and another in a future that no one seems to comprehend. Recently over lunch I was rebuked by a French friend and neighbor who had no use for my small-is-beautiful view of France. "It's not by patchwork with little organic producers in their vineyards that France will build its future," he said. He seemed to spit out the words for "little" and "organic": *petits, bio*.

I was stunned by the force of his reaction. On one level he is right. France is, after all, an industrial power with sixty million mouths to feed.

"France doesn't need to be the Switzerland of the world," he went on.

I fired back: "What about France being the *France* of the world?"

Wine and the world, after all, are better off because there is France—a France that exists outside of Paris or, for that matter, Bordeaux.

And that, friends, is something worth toasting.

ONE

Rebel with a Château

FINDING A MATTRESS IN SAINT-ÉMILION wasn't easy. The world's largest wine convention was about to descend on the city of Bordeaux, and vacant rooms in the legendary wine-growing village about twenty-five miles to the northeast seemed almost as rare as, say, Cheval Blanc '47.

Then I got lucky with a telephone lead. One bed-and-breakfast owner—who had no vacancy herself—said she had a neighbor who might have a free room just outside the vineyards of Saint-Émilion.

"Are you very big, monsieur?" Madame asked politely in French.

"Pardon?" I asked.

She explained that her neighbor was "perfectly charming," but there was one slight problem: the beds at his place were . . . on the small side.

"Well," she concluded, after I explained that I was approximately 180 centimeters (5 feet 11 inches) tall, "you could always sleep on a diagonal . . ."

I called and booked.

A week later as I drove toward my room at Château de Lescaneaut, I began having second thoughts. What had I gotten myself into? A hobbit hotel? A closet under the stairs? It was only when I turned off the main road after Saint-Émilion and entered the vines of the Côtes de Castillon that my doubts began to dissolve.

Château de Lescaneaut nestles in the flat vineyards along the banks of the Dordogne River, just a few kilometers from the site of the last battle of the Hundred Years' War. Castillon-la-Bataille,

2. François des Ligneris, in the Corbières

now a dreary village largely populated by North African immigrant
families, was the site of the battle in 1453 in which French forces
definitively drove the British (to the dismay of locals) out of Bordeaux and western France.

As it turned out, the place was almost everything I like in a country
inn—even if the bathroom towels were as rough as sandpaper and
the plumbing brayed like an overwrought donkey. The 300-year-
old farmhouse remained unchanged for generations with its creaky
wood floors, country bourgeois décor, and canopied beds so small
that my feet dangled over the edge and so high you needed a step
stool to climb in. The château was presided over by a witty, world-
weary proprietor, François Faytout Garamond, who inherited the
place from his grandfather.

As for the wine of the château, Faytout Garamond had long since
retired. He now left the work of toiling in the vines to his young,
strapping son-in-law, while he let out the five upstairs rooms to
tourists and padded around in a pair of *babouches* (slippers), a

habit from his years of living in Morocco. At the massive table in front of the hearth in the dining room, he joined his small number of guests for a breakfast of homemade cakes and jams under a series of large family oil portraits. "That's where I like my family," Faytout Garamond remarked, "on the walls."

The first morning at breakfast Faytout Garamond's clientele included me alone. He rarely accepted guests during Vinexpo, as he had no use for rowdy conventioneers. I had only made it in, presumably, because Madame *la voisine* (neighbor) had already sized me up. And knowing that I was a journalist, Faytout Garamond immediately took it upon himself to educate me on the local landscape.

"The people around here are called *l'aristocratie du bouchon* [the aristocracy of the cork]," he said. Faytout Garamond was referring to Bordeaux in general and to the elites of Saint-Émilion specifically. Just in case I might miss the double entendre of the term, he made a point of noting exactly where the collective cork rests: "In their asses," he said, using his thumb as a visual device. "The people here," he went on, "are like this . . ." His long hands went up to the side of his head to illustrate horse blinders. "And *attention*!" he warned. "They drink too much." As for Saint-Émilion itself, there was little good to be said about what it had become: "It's Marrakech!" he sniffed.

Over the course of several days I listened to his view of a world that from his vantage was going to hell in a hurry. While he had little good to say about his own countrymen, Faytout Garamond had worse things to say about the Dutch. The entire population of the Netherlands, he informed me, was forever banned from his premises—the result of one young drunk who had brought back two hookers from Bordeaux to entertain himself in one of those tiny beds. Faytout Garamond says he was compelled to boot out the trio at 3 a.m., telling them to "go sleep under a bridge."

During one morning of conversation during my weeklong stay (punctuated at regular intervals by Faytout Garamond sighing, "What is there to write about Saint-Émilion that hasn't already been written? I don't know . . . "), I said was going to meet François des Ligneris, the owner of Château Soutard in Saint-Émilion. As it turned out, des Ligneris was a relative by marriage; his wife was Faytout Garamond's niece. "François really is a cultivated young man. Educated, well traveled, very open. He's part of the aristocracy, but he's *not really* at all like them," Faytout Garamond said. He fell silent. Then, with a look I took for worry, he added: "He does like to talk a lot . . . perhaps too much."

Saint-Émilion, at first glance, is one of those ancient villages that are almost too perfect—from its postcard panoramas and picturesque plazas filled with tables in summer, to the strangely disconcerting absence of anything that might be considered bad taste. Set into a steep limestone hillside, Saint-Émilion fills a natural amphitheater topped by a plateau with vineyards that run to the edge of the horizon. A bell tower and an old dungeon dominate the high ground, and looming over the plaza below is a stone mass containing a grand troglodyte church and catacombs carved by monks who trailed the real Émilion from Brittany twelve hundred years ago.

Some winegrowing areas have history, culture, and architecture; others have charm or natural beauty; and some just have that rare combination of climate and soils that tends to produce some of the world's great wines. Saint-Émilion seemingly has it all, which explains why the vineyards spreading over Saint-Émilion and its seven neighboring villages became the first winegrowing area on UNESCO's list of world heritage sites.

Wine tourists flock here by the thousands, soaking up an afternoon of the good life and warming up their credit cards at wine shops lined up like luxury boutiques that promise worldwide shipping in a half-dozen languages. If Saint-Émilion lacks anything, it may be a soul. Scratch beneath the surface and everywhere—including under hundreds of acres of vineyards—Saint-Émilion is a giant subterranean gruyère of caves and tunnels hand dug over centuries to excavate the large white limestone blocks used to build Bordeaux and the region's châteaux. Scratch into the veneer of Saint-Émilion's *grand cru* image and you also find one of the world's most combative arenas for wine.

Saint-Émilion has some eight hundred dry red winemakers working vineyards that are small by Bordeaux standards. A "château" can refer to anything from a country manor assembled from a medieval village to a prefab house with vines just behind the kids' swing set. All Saint-Émilion wines are made from hand-harvested merlot, cabernet franc, and cabernet sauvignon grapes, but the similarities stop there. In a country that is mad for classifying things, Saint-Émilion has one of France's most meticulous classification systems. Basic wines are labeled Saint-Émilion or, better, Saint-Émilion *grand cru*. The wines that meet the highest standards over time—generally from châteaux on the high ground around Saint-Émilion village—are classified as Saint-Émilion *grand cru classé* or the ultimate, Saint-Émilion *premier grand cru classé*. Even this last category is divided in two: group A, an exclusive class of two including Cheval Blanc and Ausone; and group B, eleven others. Unlike the Medoc to the west on the other side (the left bank) of the Gironde River, where classifications change about every century, Saint-Émilion's wine classification is now revisited every ten years. Following the last review in 2006, four demoted châteaux filed suit, and a Bordeaux court suspended Saint-Émilion's wine hierarchy until further notice—resulting in an unresolved dispute that could drag on for years.

Generally, the most highly rated wines are clustered around the high ground of the sun-exposed, well-drained slopes and plateau around the village of Saint-Émilion, where wine châteaux were built in the eighteenth century. The most pedestrian wines tend to be down on the plain below Saint-Émilion. In few places is the meaning of the term "the folks on the hill" more evident. Saint-Émilion's aristocracy of the cork formed a tight circle protected by the leaders of its Jurade. The Jurade was originally a medieval council that presided over Saint-Émilion. It was reestablished after World War II to promote local wine interests—its members dressing in distinctive red clerical robes and caps along with white, hooded capes. Yet in the latter decades of the twentieth century, the folks on the hill changed. Ever-increasing wine prices for grands crus led to a huge spike in land prices. With estates so highly valued and facing inheritance battles and taxes, one by one, the old aristocracy began selling out to investor groups and wealthy outsiders.

At the same time, it was here in the 1990s that the so-called garage wine (*garagiste*) movement was born. Garagistes such as the wine merchant Jean-Luc Thunevin seized the wine world's attention and, encouraged by the oohs and aahs of Robert Parker, produced small quantities of superconcentrated wines from what was considered less than noble terroir down on the plain. Garage wines turned hot. And by the end of the millennium, they were selling for more than wines from the region's elite châteaux, which in turn began producing their own "garage"-style wines. It was only a matter of time before *garagiste* became synonymous with *opportuniste*.

After the *garagistes* came the *arriviste*—Gérard Perse, the wealthy self-made businessman and greengrocer who began buying up Saint-Émilion châteaux as if they were heads of lettuce on market day. Perse didn't engender himself to locals when he bought Château Pavie, one of the most prized jewels of Saint-Émilion, and said it wasn't difficult upping the quality. Team Perse used a supercharged garage-type formula, spiked prices, and won the devotion of Parker ("some of the most flamboyant and seductive clarets in Saint-Émilion").

In the spring of 2004, Parker's advocacy of Pavie turned personal after British author and *Financial Times* critic Jancis Robinson released her blind tasting notes of Pavie 2003, calling it "porty sweet" and a "ridiculous wine more reminiscent of a late-harvest zinfandel than a red Bordeaux." A war of words ensued. Parker, who judged the wine an "off the chart effort" (95-100 score!), un-characteristically went on the offensive, writing, "These comments are very much in keeping with the nasty swipes at all the Pavies made by Perse and mirror the comments of . . . the reactionaries in Bordeaux." On her Web site, Robinson shot back, "Am I not allowed to have my own opinion?"

I drank Pavie, along with the rest of Perse's wines, at an orga-nized tasting with the Perses in Cannes in the spring of 2005. I sampled every year of Pavie from 1998 to 2004 and found them simultaneously delicious and repulsive. They were armed with sweet fruit and tannins like missiles that exploded horizontally across the tongue and into your cheeks and gums—the gustatory equivalent of Pamela Anderson, a big "wow" effect that was hard to take in anything but small doses. Pavie, it seemed to me, was good for turning heads in the street, but not for a relationship that would last more than a glass or two. There was also something that left a bad aftertaste, and it wasn't the unruly tannins. It wasn't just the price either, although the "monster" Pavie 2000 was selling in France for more than $300 a bottle. While Perse and his wife, Chantal, seemed like perfectly nice people, it seemed to me there was something tasteless about the way Perse portrayed his wine as an extension of his own power. A slick kit handed out at the tasting featured a full-page glossy photographic image of Perse with this question: "Has Gérard Perse discovered the Holy Grail—or has he simply set a new standard?" Were we talking about red wine here or rocket fuel for masters of the universe?

Now, in 2005, the man who seemed to be most intent on shaking up Saint-Émilion was neither a garagiste nor an outsider, but one of the cork aristocracy's own.

From the outside, Château Soutard was a majestic, if slightly faded, eighteenth-century limestone manor on the plateau north of Saint-Émilion, producing fine grand cru classé wine. The château was built in the centuries-old farming hamlet of Soutard by a meticulous winegrower by the name of Jean Combret de Faurie, who at about the same time planted some fifty-four acres of vines within an enclosure of low walls.

At the beginning of the nineteenth century, the estate was sold, eventually passing by marriage and inheritance directly into the des Ligneris family of counts and countesses. During World War II the château was occupied by German officers, and though des Ligneris's father, the count Jacques des Ligneris, never talked about the war to his children, the Nazis left their mark. In the antique woodwork of the kitchen hearth, one officer inscribed in German in ornate gothic type: "In our will is our victory."

At the close of a lean decade following the war, François des Ligneris was born on the fourteenth of July (Bastille Day), but in aristocratic tradition his birth date was declared as the thirteenth. Now at fifty, after working at Soutard his entire adult life and controlling it for more than a decade, François des Ligneris was an unlikely revolutionary. Yet des Ligneris was publicly ridiculing as a charade the seventy-year-old French wine appellation system—the very same system that maintained the status of his family estate. He helped found a group of winemakers known as SEVE (a reference to the "sap" that is the life force of vines), who called themselves *paysans-vignerons* (farmer or peasant winemakers); they were asking for the transformation of French winemaking along environmental, ethical, and certain esoteric lines, with the stated goal of defying standardization. They called for the elimination of the use of herbicides, pesticides, and soil disinfectant (which des Ligneris noted did not exist at the time of the creation of the appellation system) along with chemical yeasts, additives, and overwrought extraction techniques. Their manifesto went so far as to call for respect for the "health and growth of those who work in the vines as well as civic and social environment" and to communicate to the consumer "in all transparency all the information concerning their work in the vines and in their cellars."

Des Ligneris upset the elite wine world of Saint-Émilion and Bordeaux with more than his ideological pronouncements. "It's on the verge of scandalous," Hubert de Boüard of Château Angélus (which, incidentally, was to be one of the luxury products consumed by James Bond in the 2006 film *Casino Royale*) told *Le Monde*. Des Ligneris's scandal? He'd begun making the most common of all wines—labeled simply *French table wine*—from vineyards he'd purchased on the other side of the Dordogne River in the Bordeaux region of Entre-deux-Mers and in the Languedoc region of Les Corbières. His Entre-deux-Mers wines had provocative names such as Vin des Promesses (Wine of Promises, which bore the inscription "Tomorrow I will stop drinking") and L'R de Rien (a wordplay that translates to "seems like nothing"). And perhaps as the final insult to the Bordeaux establishment, des Ligneris didn't want the name Bordeaux anywhere on the bottles he produced in Bordeaux—bottles that he fitted with a screwcap instead of a cork.

I met des Ligneris in his office, part of a large old farmhouse at Soutard. My first impression was of a man with a slightly portly build, salt-and-pepper hair, a close-cropped beard, and gray-green eyes that shone with the serene, playful expression of a yogi. "I am very bothersome for the people who run things in Saint-Émilion," des Ligneris said with no prompting. He sat at an enormous wood table, which, like every other inch of furniture or floor, was covered with stacks of paper, books, and bottles of wine. It was a hot period in Saint-Émilion, but des Ligneris (as a matter of some aristocratic habit) did not wear short sleeves. He wore an ironed, long-sleeved, striped shirt, dark khakis, and webbed sandals. He calmly recounted what he thought of the people running things in Saint-Émilion and Bordeaux.

"They disinfect their soils until they are dead, they mix vintages, add acids and bacteria. They do everything. It is a scandal." The words spilled out so easily, it was obvious he'd been down this road before. He went on: "At first when the appellations were created, they were a good idea. But now the labels of wine are a great masquerade."

Des Ligneris then took a pen and drew on the back of an envelope a series of long rectangles and small squares. The small squares, he explained, represented the wine in barrels that some châteaux present "for tastings and the journalists," while the large rectangles represented a totally different wine that was destined for consumers. "I know this happens because I know a lot of people who work in the châteaux," he said, adding that at the root of the trickery was a seemingly inexhaustible appetite for luxury brands. "The nouveaux riches in Russia, China, and Japan will spend no matter what to show off. They buy the watch, they buy the car, they buy the girl . . . and they want to buy the wine. It is all about putting distance between themselves and other people." I figured he was either too gracious or too tactful to lump wealthy Americans in that group.

Des Ligneris produced more papers, among them a chart showing the steep rise in wine prices of some of his aristocratic neighbors leading up to and beyond the year 2000 millennial vintage. In 1999 much of the plateau and hillsides of Saint-Émilion was hit by a devastating hailstorm. In that year des Ligneris christened his L'R de Rien wine as a way of using the storm-damaged grapes in a cheaper table wine. Des Ligneris pulled out copies of government records from the time showing that one of the most prestigious châteaux in Saint-Émilion had actually increased its production after it was hit by the storm. "How," des Ligneris asked, "is that possible?" With tens of millions of euros at stake, he said, there was only one conclusion: greed had found a way to work miracles.

We crossed the wide dirt and gravel courtyard at Soutard, and, as if excusing himself, des Ligneris stated the obvious: "I am an idealist."

I have been to many wine châteaux where the main purpose of public spaces was to impress visitors. Down the road at Angélus there are pictures of heads of state and movie stars. At Cheval Blanc a massive painting of a white horse was hung for the visit of Russian president Vladimir Putin. But in the room at the entry to Soutard's winemaking operations, the whitewashed walls were blank. Off to the right was tacked one piece of plain white paper—on it was printed a French translation of a poem by the Italian poet Claudio Parmiggiani:

March 5, 1953
March 5, 1953: Stalin's funeral: immense crowd.
March 5, 1953: Prokofiev's funeral: twenty persons.

Obscure poets, I would learn, were a specialty of des Ligneris, who then pointed to the long empty wall in front of the entrance. "I tell people who come to visit that this is a map of Soutard," he said abstractly, and then added as an aside: "I tell them that as a way to get them to leave the materialistic world behind." Des Ligneris, sticking to this tangent, conjured images of winemaking as a sort of sacred ritual. Even the picking of grapes, he noted, bending at the knee and waist for emphasis, required a sort of genuflection—as in prayer.

In front of that wall was a narrow table with neatly arrayed objects: jars of various sizes containing soil, vine cuttings, grapes preserved in alcohol, a set of large springs, and a basket containing a whistle, a wooden faucet, light bulbs, and more. For the next forty-five minutes, he launched into a sort of performance piece, using the props to illustrate his brand of noninterventionist winemaking philosophy in which humans are "the small bridges that allow the two stories of the earth and sky to be together."

What distinguished des Ligneris's winemaking was his meticulous attention to detail. When it was time to replant vines, he waited seven years after ripping up the old vines in order to let the soils rejuvenate. Common rites of spring such as stripping vines of excess leaves and fruit were, to des Ligneris, an unnecessary practice if the plant was in balance. To circulate wine in his stainless steel vats during fermentation—a common process of taking the liquid on the bottom and watering the cap of skins and seeds that forms on top—des Ligneris used gentle peristaltic pumps. Like most fine French winemakers, he added no yeasts—allowing only the naturally occurring yeasts in the grapes to start fermentation—and used a minimum of sulfur (or sulfites to kill bacteria and preserve the wine). After fermentation, only a small percentage of his wood barrels used to raise his wine were new and he used varied sizes—other than the relatively small fifty-nine-gallon Bordeaux *barrique*—to limit the influence of the wood on the wine. In the early 1990s, after research showed that traces of chlorine in wood treatments and building materials could escape into the air, he went on a crusade that other family members found excessive: replacing the wood beams holding up the roof of the winery, recovering the walks with lime wash, and installing an elaborate water-filtering system. Yet for all his purism, des Ligneris has refused to encamp himself with the growing number of organic winegrowers. He insisted that in some cases he would rather use a limited amount of "neutral" synthetic treatment for sick vines than organic sulfur, which would have more of an adverse effect on the insects in his vineyard. It quickly became apparent that des Ligneris was such an independent thinker he couldn't belong to anyone else's club.

At the end of his demonstration, des Ligneris picked up a strainer filled with more props and announced, "These things illustrate the wines I do not make." He pulled out a small builder's level. "I don't make perfect wines," he says. "I don't make uniform wines . . ." Then out came more props and with them more metaphors: a file, a folding ruler, a little pink dog collar, a calculator.

We headed out to lunch in des Ligneris's well-worn Renault sedan. As we were getting in the car, I noticed an old man about forty yards away in front of the old château. He seemed to be intently staring in our direction. I stared back. "My father," des Ligneris said. Oddly, neither man made a wave or a gesture in the other's direction. Des Ligneris drove away from him down the gravel entry road, and I could feel the old count—who was once known locally as the Comte Rouge (Red Count) for his Socialist Party activities— still standing and staring.

Lunch was at des Ligneris's restaurant/wine bar in Saint-Émilion. Naturally, it had a suggestive name: l'Envers du Décor (the other side of the picture). We sat on the shaded terrace in back nestled between the restaurant and a small chapel. I ordered the daily specials—a small cake of beef tail, followed by a side of roasted black pork. We drank one of des Ligneris's light white table wines, which he said he was making for "my freedom of expression." And in between periods in which des Ligneris stood to greet friends and winemakers, or discuss the house cuisine, this father of three daughters softly continued his indictment against the Bordeaux wine establishment.

"Even the words used to describe wine are frightening," des Ligneris said. "*Selection, concentration* . . . they remind you of something, don't they?" Des Ligneris gave me a meaningful look. People this obsessed are usually bores, I thought. But, on the contrary, I found des Ligneris immediately likeable and fascinating—perhaps the most charismatic winemaker I'd met.

In the weeks after our meeting, I thought often about our conversations, trying to figure him out. Was he a revolutionary for wanting to overturn the status quo of winemaking in Bordeaux? A reactionary trying to turn back the clock? Or a monk trying to keep the brotherhood pure? Was he a bohemian or a traditionalist? Paysan or intellectual? Artist or entrepreneur? Crazed or sane? It seemed to me that des Ligneris was a man living out his complex contradictions to their hilt. Had it not been for Château Soutard and for the estate manager's moving away at a time his father's health was failing in the 1970s, things might have turned out differently.

Des Ligneris explained how he had completed the initial stages of architectural study, then, after his obligatory military service at a naval-air base in Hyères, returned home to work at Soutard, which his father had arranged for him and his two sisters to inherit directly from their grandmother in 1979. Though the property belonged to the siblings, the father remained the winegrower and producer. Over his first decade, he said, he worked for his father at a rate of pay lower than that of most of the workers. At the same time, des Ligneris indulged his artistic side, cultivating a circle of friends made of artists, writers, and musicians.

Hanging behind the bar at l'Envers du Décor was one of several posters that des Ligneris had conceived, printed, and distributed as part of his free expression. This particular poster was entitled *Vis Parker* (which translates, literally, to "Screw Parker"). The central illustration was a screw chart of five Phillips head screws. Under each was a number in bold—Parker ratings on his famous 100-point scale. Beneath each number was a series of quotes from Parker's French translations. Des Ligneris made the point of saying a co-collaborator assembled these, as he himself doesn't read wine critics. (Nor, he added, does he own a television, snow ski, or take winter vacations in the Seychelles.) Among the assembled terms for wines with 90-plus Parker scores were "stupéfiant de concentration" (astounding concentration), "véritable monstre" (veritable monster) "arômes de vitamine" (aromas of vitamin), "quintessence de puissance" (quintessence of power), and "notes élégantes de ketchup" (elegant notes of ketchup).

"I think that Parker is intellectually honest," des Ligneris said. "He has an opinion and he expresses it. But I think he's been exploited by the people of Bordeaux who fix wine samples and the others who do what they can to please him."

Incidentally, Parker has had good things to say about Soutard. Although he hasn't ranked it with his Saint-Émilion favorites, such as Angélus, Cheval Blanc, the Perse wines, and Valandraud, he refers to Soutard in the fourth edition of his *Bordeaux* as "a serious traditionally made wine that usually repays one's patience."

Early that evening I returned to Soutard and found des Ligneris in the area of the winery where he had stored cases of wine going back more than a decade. Des Ligneris and two other men sat on wine crates, wine glasses in hand. One of des Ligneris's guests was Arnaud Daudier de Cassini, a young, earnest winemaker who had a few acres of vines around his house on the plain below Saint-Émilion. Daudier de Cassini made his wine in what had been a home garage, but like most young winemakers he had no interest in calling himself a garagiste.

Des Ligneris brought me a glass and then poured a variety of wines, including his new table wines, some peripatetic experiments, and several vintages of Soutard. I took no notes and didn't spit. What I remember about Soutard is its subtlety. Certain years were meatier, bigger, and more tannic, and others more elegant—lighter with a hint of acid that made them last longer in the mouth. These were not in-your-face wines that spontaneously made you pucker and say wow. They were wines that would take time to get to know.

At one point des Ligneris rummaged around in some crates and pulled out a pair of bottles containing barrel samples of what became part of the mix of the 2000 Soutard. The first was a sample of wine raised in acacia wood barrels—an experiment des Ligneris began after he read that the ancient Egyptians had used acacia for such purposes. I stuck my nose in the glass and quickly recoiled. In those first seconds, I smelled what can only be described as cat box odor, though that aroma gradually dissipated. The second sample was made from cabernet franc raised in new oak. Here was something you could recognize immediately—a big, roasted, tannic feel that attacked the gums and cheeks.

"I can't drink this," Daudier de Cassini said as he got up and poured the contents of his glass down a floor drain. "I'm sorry."

"I do this," des Ligneris said, explaining why he kept barrel samples, "to confront the enemy. . . . I could make a wine like this . . ." Des Ligneris opened another bottle and said something cryptic about making walls disappear by facing the wall. He spoke of threats that been implied to him and of conspiracies in the Bordeaux establishment. Recently, he said, a government auditor had told him that he was being audited because "you talk too much."

I wasn't always sure what he was talking about, but I was certain that des Ligneris was a man who cared very deeply about wine and the legacy he would leave. In des Ligneris I found a new element of terroir that I hadn't yet considered, but that should count for something: here was a man who didn't possess the land on which he was born so much as he loved it.

About a year and a half later I met des Ligneris under entirely different circumstances: Soutard had been sold. It was an indication of how common a story it had become that the sale of one of the most venerable names in Saint-Émilion to the insurance group La Mondiale (for a price estimated at 35 million euros) barely merited a footnote in the world wine press. I phoned des Ligneris, who outlined an all-too-familiar story among France's family dynasties. His two sisters, both younger and neither of whom worked, had wanted to cash out.

"There was no way I could afford to buy their shares," des Ligneris said, insisting that it had all turned out for the best. He had finally found freedom. And he was redoubling his winemaking efforts elsewhere, particularly in the Corbières. "I am making a table wine without herbicides, without chemicals, without yeasts, without adding bacteria or acids or anything. Why?" he asked. "Because the *grands châteaux* of Bordeaux are making their wines with herbicides and chemicals, with yeasts and with bacteria and everything else."

Two weeks later I was on a train for Bordeaux to meet des Ligneris and learn more about his plans and his new-found freedom away from Saint-Émilion. When he met me outside the station that evening, he came striding up in jeans and a rumpled linen jacket. I noticed that his paunch had grown, shifting his center of gravity closer to the earth.

After our *bonjours*, his next words were unforgettable. He thanked me profusely for coming to see him, then added: "It's incredible the number of people who don't want to have anything to do with me now that I don't have Soutard." With those first words, I immediately had the sense that des Ligneris's manner had changed. He seemed less ethereal than I had remembered him. As he bounded down the steps of the parking garage by the train station, he explained he had a stop to make in Bordeaux before we made our way to Saint-Émilion—delivering a few cases of wine to a friend. I noticed his shoes hitting the pavement; they were worn leather boat shoes with red laces that looked as though they had been improvised from string.

Bordeaux was covered in a light mist. The limestone buildings facing the port and the bridges crossing the Gironde were lit to show off the city's restoration after years of decay. The new white Christmas lights above the city boulevards made the point that Bordeaux had bounced back. As he drove a panel truck through those streets, des Ligneris elaborated on the sale of Soutard. His sisters had wanted to sell for twelve years, and more recently they gave him an ultimatum to buy them out or risk that they would sell a controlling interest out from under him.

"One of my sisters told me, 'I don't want to do it . . . I prefer to keep it in the family. . . .' It was like somebody pointing a gun at you and saying, 'I don't want to shoot you.' Well, if you don't want to shoot, then don't pull the trigger."

Des Ligneris parked in a row of cars on a side street, then went around the side of the van and slid the panel door open. I got out and helped him carry several wine cases up a set of stairs and into the entrance of a grand bourgeois townhouse. A slightly older, smartly dressed woman greeted us in the hall. Des Ligneris and the woman exchanged the traditional French kiss-kiss on each cheek. We got the rest of the cases from the van and set them down in the hall. After des Ligneris exchanged a kiss-kiss *au revoir*, we were off.

As we drove back to Saint-Émilion, a light rain began to fall. Des Ligneris described how, once he realized he was outvoted by his sisters, he took charge of fetching the best price for Soutard. He said his talks with La Mondiale were followed by intrigue among competing investor groups and other Bordeaux châteaux who tried to scare off La Mondiale and drive down des Ligneris's price by discrediting Soutard. He said obliquely that the Saint-Émilion winegrowers association and France's wine oversight agency, Institut National des Appellations d'Origine (INAO), had been dragged into the affair. But, he added, he signed a promise to La Mondiale not to sue those agencies or discuss any interference in the sale. "When you are independent," he said, "you have to pay *très, très cher*. And they bought my silence."

Over dinner at l'Envers du Décor, we drank des Ligneris's latest efforts from the Corbières in the Languedoc. Not surprisingly, they were all labeled table wines that bucked the trend in the Corbières appellation, which had limited the use of carignan grapes to 50 percent of the final blend that goes into the bottle. In other words, for a wine to bear the mark of the Corbières appellation, at least half of the blend had to come from other grapes, typically grenache and syrah. Perhaps it was snobbism on the part of the appellation leaders or an effort to break with the Languedoc's past. Carignan was long the staple there—a hot-dry climate grape that was used to produce seas of strong but otherwise characterless buy-in-bulk red.

By insisting on using about 70 percent carignan in his three cuvées, des Ligneris was obliged to label his wine as table wine—the most pedestrian of classifications. At the same time, des Ligneris was free to make wine as he pleased. The first two bottles were fitted with screwcaps and were called Zinzin (colloquial for "crazy") with a label depicting a matador and a bear, and Notre Dame de Consolation, named after a chapel on a hillside from which the grapes for that wine came. Because table wines are also not allowed to show vintages des Ligneris discreetly indicated to consumers that these wines were from the 2003 *millesime* (vintage) by printing "03" on his corks or hiding those numbers in fine print on the label.

The third wine, des Ligneris's new prestige cuvée, was called Arazime (the word for "grape" in Languedocian) and came from des Ligneris's best parcels. The wine was partially aged in oak barrels and the bottles had real corks. All three wines were well finished and demonstrated in degrees what can be done with carignan when it's grown and worked with care. The result often combines the unmistakable flavor of black pepper with the scent of fresh tobacco—an in-glass experience that people tend to either love or hate.

We ate roast pigeon and drank the Arazime. I asked des Ligneris what it had been like to lose Soutard. He set down his fork and knife. "It's a subject I haven't really discussed. Not even with my wife," he said. "I think of the writer Henri Calet: 'Ne me secouez pas. Je suis plein de larmes' [Don't shake me. I am full of tears]."

I slept that night in a guest room above the wine bar. The next day began with a warm brilliant morning that felt more like September than December. The light after the rain was crystalline—making the plateau of Saint-Émilion seem that much closer to heaven. Des Ligneris came by the bar early and we walked out to the town's southeast edge—where des Ligneris had bought a series of buildings— partially renovated ruins from which he planned to reconstitute his base in Saint-Émilion.

His new mailing address was 1 Rue de Liberté. Freedom Street. "I didn't think of that until months after I bought the place," des Ligneris said. He showed me a series of gutted apartments that he planned to renovate into offices overlooking Saint-Émilion and the vineyards to the south and west—away from Soutard.

Later that morning we stopped by the house des Ligneris had lived in all his adult life—a winemaker's cottage on the Soutard estate that he had renovated twenty years earlier. The vineyards spread in every direction. I looked towards the monumental building with white shutters where des Ligneris's parents still lived. Under the arrangements of the sale, des Ligneris's parents would have to leave the château, but des Ligneris kept the cottage. Chickens ran around in a pen out back. A stable next door housed the family's two donkeys. This wasn't how I'd expect the owner of grand wine château to live, but then des Ligneris no longer had a château. In America, few millionaires lived so close to the earth. In Saint-Émilion, des Ligneris was one of the last.

A wood porch led to a simple wood door, which led into a kitchen built around a large fireplace and a long, heavy wood table. The signs of family life were everywhere: the piles of coats and shoes packed into cubbies by the door, the photos of his daughters tacked to a bulletin board, the dishes and bread from breakfast still on the table. Down some stairs off to the left was a larger room with a tall ceiling and wood beams. It had once served as a dining room, now it was used to store part of des Ligneris collection of modern paintings.

Des Ligneris grabbed a black satchel from another room. We made our way outside to a Volvo station wagon by the house. The car looked and smelled brand new and was outfitted with all manner of electronics that its owner had not learned to operate. A luxury, des Ligneris noted, the first new car he had bought in a long while.

Des Ligneris swung the car down from the plateau as we crossed the village of Saint-Émilion. In a matter of minutes we crossed the Dordogne River and entered into Entre-deux-Mers. Des Ligneris showed me his vines and the storehouse he had purchased all around the little river port town of Cabara. The only problem with this region, des Ligneris said, was that as picturesque as the landscape was—with its turreted hilltop châteaux, intimate villages, the precision stands of poplar trees along stream banks, and its vibrant green prairies with handsome cattle—the vineyards were not truly great. The soils were in fact too rich and productive to produce the kind of exceptional terroir that would make a great wine. "You will see," des Ligneris repeated more than once.

As he drove on, des Ligneris talked about his disillusionment with Bordeaux, from the middlemen or *negociants* to the winemaking practices. He spoke of the repeated scandals of wine houses that had cut their wine with cheaper wine from other regions or countries. "So what does it mean to put Bordeaux on my label?" he asked. "I don't want to be part of a family in which I can't stand what's going on in the family," he said. "I want to say, *non, non*, and *non!*"

As we got on the autoroute and headed south toward Toulouse, des Ligneris talked about his family, its history and its secrets. He and his father—the man who I remembered as staring at us so oddly that spring day at Soutard—had not spoken for years. The count, despite his socialist political tendencies, never accepted that his son had chosen to wed the daughter of a coal seller. And so the count removed himself, choosing not even to attend his grandchildren's baptisms. At Soutard, des Ligneris said, his role had been simply to provide for his siblings and to make sure the monthly check arrived on time.

Outside, the sky had turned gray. After Toulouse the landscape changed again to red rocky hillsides, low scrub brush, and olives, and des Ligneris's mood seemed to brighten. He lowered his window, and through diesel fuel I could smell the sea and the south and the dust and the faint smells of the *garrigue*—the Mediterranean basin landscape of scrub and wild herbs.

In a matter of hours we had changed worlds, as different from each other as New England and New Mexico. In Saint-Émilion every centimeter of space seemed to have been scrutinized, cultivated, refined. We were entering a world where the horizon was wild and mountainous, and the land was as dry as northern Spain, where any right turn would have taken us.

"We are going to do in the Corbières," des Ligneris said, "what is impossible in Bordeaux . . . impossible because in Bordeaux there isn't enough pure, natural space." We turned off the autoroute after the medieval tourist city of Carcassone and headed into the heart of the heretic countryside. Road signs don't let you forget that you are in the Pays de Cathares, named for the Christian religious sect that once proliferated under the protection of the counts of Toulouse and that held a very harsh view of the Catholic Church and the material world. The Cathars paid dearly—*très, très cher*—for their independence and were exterminated in a series of crusades and the Inquisition in the thirteenth century. It seemed a fitting setting for a refugee from Saint-Émilion.

The Languedoc is one of France's largest winegrowing regions, with a reputation as the country's most mediocre. Wines from these fertile sunbaked plains were produced by cooperatives by the tanker-load sent off to quench the thirst of France's miners and armies. At the beginning of the twenty-first century, the Languedoc was hurting more than any other French wine region. Cooperatives were paying less and less for grapes to make wine that went unsold.

Many winegrowers were abandoning their work, finding it more lucrative to take the government subsidies to tear up their vines. But even as wine and land prices fell, outsiders such as des Ligneris moved in, buying up select vineyards. What most interested des Ligneris was what he called his *terroir d'exception*. He sought out the prime spots on the plateaus of the Corbières, the range of low mountains jutting north from the eastern Pyrenees. A maxim of fine Old World winemaking is that great wines come from poor soils. The rich soils of the plains are fine for producing quantities of grapes, but it is the high ground, the well-exposed rocky slopes and plateaus, where vines send deep roots in search of water and minerals. In France and most of Europe's appellations, irrigation is generally forbidden or is so expensive it's out of the question. Vines under such stress produce grapes that are less abundant, but more concentrated in flavors and aromas that reflect the soil and environment.

This was as true in Saint-Émilion as it was here. The difference was that prime vineyards in Saint-Émilion cost about 600,000 euros an acre. Here, in the relatively unscouted Corbières, they cost less than 5,000. And des Ligneris was on a spending spree.

We stopped at des Ligneris's winery in Fabrezon, a typically bleak-in-winter village with a couple of cafés and a local wine cooperative with huge petroleum-sized tanks for wine in its backyard. It was here des Ligneris had renovated a small old winery—fitting it with a pair of rows of square gray cement wine vats from a Burgundy producer who used spring water to mix the cement. We were greeted by des Ligneris's local manager and cellar master, Fabrice Eygreteau, a forty-year-old Bordeaux native with a long pointed nose and melancholy brown eyes, who had spent most of his working life in Saint-Émilion and had followed des Ligneris here.

The three of us got into one of two old blue Gendarmerie vans—absent the letters and flashing lights—that des Ligneris had purchased for his new wine operation. Des Ligneris drove, heading north. Somehow lunch had passed us by, but des Ligneris was determined that we should climb into the hills before the afternoon darkness fell.

In the nearby town of La Talairane, we saw a pair of young gendarmes—a woman and a man—by the side of the road. They watched as the old blue van approached, and waved des Ligneris over to the side. Des Ligneris, smiling and with impeccable manners, informed them that he did not have the papers for the vehicle with him—an offense that could have resulted in a very long afternoon in custody.

"Have you been drinking today?" the young man asked, looking the three of us over. In an area such as this with an abundance of unsellable wine and little work, this was not an unreasonable question.

"Not today," des Ligneris smiled.

Just the same, the young man produced a cellophane pouch with a plastic tube and balloon attached and had des Ligneris blow into it. He scrutinized the results of the alcohol breath analysis, warned des Ligneris about not carrying his proper papers, and sent us on our way. We crossed rivers and creeks and small canyons carved into rock that changed from pink to gray to yellow. Then we turned onto a road that zigzagged up the steep hillside, and continued after the pavement gave way to dirt and rocks through a forest of pine, scrub oaks, and brambles. We banged around inside the van as the axles seemed to be straining. And we emerged onto a plateau of ten acres of winter-bare Grenache vines planted with a soil laced with shards of flat schistic rock. We had climbed more than a thousand feet to this place, and off at the ends of the plateau in every direction were stands of cypress and untamed garrigue.

As I pushed open the door of the van with my shoulder, I was hit with an explosion of aromas. I looked down. We had parked in a sprawling patch of wild thyme. As we walked, I could see that every bit of red dirt and rock that was uncultivated was sprouting wild asparagus, lavender, rosemary, and fennel, whose scents mingled in a warm, moist wind from the south.

"Here," des Ligneris said emphatically, "You can talk about organic. There are no neighbors dumping chemicals in their soil, because there are no neighbors. Here the only neighbors are the sky and the garrigue."

Later that evening the weather began to change, sending a chill through the Corbières. By 7 p.m. in Fabrezon, the only creatures stirring on the shuttered streets were cats. Before our half-hour drive to a restaurant near Carcassone, we tasted some of the young red wines in des Ligneris's vats, samples of what would go into the final Arazime cuvée. The wines were—to the surprise of all of us but most of all to Eygreteau, who had tasted them all two days earlier—bitter and overly acidic in a way the French call *nerveux* (nervous). After the fourth sample, des Ligneris stuck out his tongue and called it something else: *chiant* (shitty). Yet he didn't seem at all concerned. I considered this a good winemaker's patience: Wines, particularly new wines, change dramatically from day to day and week to week, along with an obvious list of environmental variables like weather and barometric pressure and some more obscure ones like the phases of the moon.

Then Eygreteau produced a bottle of light limpid yellow wine— an experiment with sauvignon blanc. The small crop of grapes had stopped fermenting before the wine was dry, presumably as the alcohol killed off the natural yeasts in the grapes. The result was a curiosity: sweet citrusy wine, lighter than a Sauternes but agreeable and easy to drink. Other winemakers might dose the 1,500 liters of sweet wine with yeast to finish fermenting the sugars, but des Ligneris was content to leave it sweet and watch how it developed, perhaps to sell what little he had as an aperitif wine. "Certainly not to please the wine professionals," he said.

Des Ligneris and I stayed that night in a small hotel that was normally closed for winter. The proprietor had left des Ligneris a key but had neglected to turn on the water heater. When I opened the bathroom faucet, it coughed, sputtered, and spit cold water over the front of my sweater.

The following morning a rude cold wind blew down from Alaric, the black mountain northwest of Fabrezon, and piled the large fallen leaves of the platane trees up high on the village sidewalks. Des Ligneris, Eygreteau, and I found coffee at the local bar, known as the Café du Théâtre. In fact, there was no theater in Fabrezon— just the local *salle des fêtes* (community center) across the street.

Inside the café, the air was thick with cigarette smoke. About a dozen unshaven men in camouflage and layers of colorless clothing gathered by the bar. As we approached, I was surprised that every one of them politely shook our hands.

The language spoken here was not the trilling *pointu* (pointed) French of Paris or the genteel private-school French of Bordeaux society. *Languedoc* comes from the term *Langue d'Oc*—the Mediterranean tongue derived from vulgar Latin and spread in the time of the Cathars across all of the southern part of France and parts of northern Italy. ("Oc" refers to the word for "yes" used among Occitan speakers, versus the "oi" of the north.) In the twentieth century the language was largely merged into French dialects pruned of fancy nasal pronunciations and diphthongs, with vowels clipped or added at will. The overall effect, at places such as the Café du Théâtre, is a guttural tongue in which the speaker could be imagined to be gnawing on unpitted olives. Multiple coffees were passed around, more men came into the bar, and there were more rounds of handshaking.

Des Ligneris seated himself at a table away from the bar with a man sporting a wild gray ponytail and an old camouflage jacket. Des Ligneris pulled out a blank piece of paper and pen from his black satchel, and the man began drawing on the paper. I watched des Ligneris, planted a few feet away in his bar chair. As it turned out, he was negotiating to buy a plot of land with a large hangar to store his tractors. His hands looked thicker than before. A hint of Languedoc sauced his words.

Eygreteau explained that he had called a local oenologist that morning and described the sudden changes in the vats of red wine. "She told me she had the same experience yesterday at one of her clients. She said that when the winds here shift from the Mediterranean to the North, the wine is completely turned upside down." (Later that morning—only sixteen hours after the last tasting—we tasted from a few of the same vats as the night before, and there was a detectable difference: some of the bitterness had retreated and the fruit flavors came to the fore.)

"Winemaking is so different here than in Saint-Émilion," Eygreteau said. "In Saint-Émilion we did everything possible to extract nature in the wine. Here we have to put the brakes on." He told me how he had approached des Ligneris about working for him several years earlier, after becoming disenchanted with Bordeaux grands crus.

"Some of the practices in the châteaux were not very clean. François is different—he's very demanding—but he's not demanding for a specific result. If the wine turns out different than what he expected, that's okay with him."

When we left the place, Eygreteau stayed in town as des Ligneris and I headed up again into the hills, where we would walk a portion of every last vineyard that belonged to him. At one point as we crossed the plain, des Ligneris stopped and waved down an older man on a tractor. Des Ligneris had bought acres of vines from this man, Jean-Claude Climent. Climent, who sold his grapes to the local cooperative, told a story of more acres of vines he was planning to pull up for the price the government was paying. "The problem here is that we know how to make wine, but we don't know how to sell wine," he said. "Nowadays you have to know how to sell wine. I don't know anything about selling wine."

Climent spoke of vineyards that he was going to rip up to collect government subsidies. Des Ligneris asked about a particular vineyard on a nearby plateau.

"Oh, I'm going to rip that up too," Climent said, offhandedly, eyeing des Ligneris.

"Don't you dare," des Ligneris said.

Climent shrugged, and mentioned that des Ligneris could buy this vineyard, if he were willing to buy some others with it. It seemed that this was part of a negotiation between the two men: Climent was holding a coveted vineyard hostage; des Ligneris was unwilling to pay the current ransom.

"If you rip up those vines, I'll never speak to you again," des Ligneris said as he climbed back in the truck. We said our goodbyes and continued up the road.

"Jean-Claude is a character," des Ligneris remarked, "but he's sly. You have to watch him. You have to be very, very careful with him."

Later that morning, we arrived at the crest of a plateau high above the valley floor and far above any vines. There was the explosive smell of wild herbs. Knee-high garrigue seemed to go on forever. Des Ligneris bounded up the hill nearly running toward an old ruin, a *bergerie* or shepherd's dwelling that had long ago been consumed by vegetation and the elements. He grinned and sucked in the air through his nose.

"Here, one is . . ." He held up his palms and made an upward flourish with his hands. Des Ligneris had bought dozens of acres of wild land here a half decade earlier. There were no vines. Which was the point. He was going to plant the hillside. We came to a pile of wood tangled with decayed vines and wire—a reminder that someone else had once given up and pulled up their vines. Yet des Ligneris was intent on staking his legacy to this spot. He believed that this hilltop would produce wine as beautiful and memorable as the place itself—not just for the next year or for five years, but for a long time thereafter.

He was telling me how this piece of land had reminded him of a poem by Jules Laforgue, the nineteenth-century French poet who had been inspired by Walt Whitman. I thought of des Ligneris planted on the bar chair that morning. I thought how far we were from the Saint-Émilion society that would most likely snicker if they saw him here now.

He turned and continued over the other side of the hill. I had to hurry to keep up with him, and somewhere along that trail I had the feeling that I was witnessing a man being born.

TWO

The Wrath of Grapes

NOT LONG INTO MY CAREER as a *vendangeur* (wine grape picker) in Alsace—about twenty minutes to be exact—I began to worry about my survival.

How I'd gotten myself entangled in the vines of the tiny winemaking village of Wolxheim, France, requires some explaining. My connection to Wolxheim was my friend Daniel Schmitt, a retired fabric salesman from nearby Molsheim who now lived in France's Sunbelt in Grasse. Daniel was my Sunday morning tennis partner: while most residents of the local countryside were sleeping off Saturday night, we were out chasing yellow balls to the cries of roosters.

Breaks in our tennis "match" were often taken up with the French custom of reviewing and recounting recent meals. Daniel's end of the conversation usually involved the cuisine and wines from his home province—for Alsatians, who often refer to their present-day countrymen in the third person as "les Français," are evangelical about Alsatian terroir.

Over the course of several years and dinners at the small apartment that was chez Schmitt, Daniel and his wife, Michelle, had introduced my wife and me to the delights of Alsace's sturdy Teutonic cuisine and the region's delicious, aromatic wines. A feast at Daniel's place might start with goose foie gras accompanied by a chilled sweet gewürztraminer or, better yet, a perfumey tokay pinot gris. (Wines in Alsace are unique in France in that they are classified principally by grape variety and not by winegrowing area.) For the main course—traditional sauerkraut with cooked sausages, ham, and stewed fat—there would be a bottle of dry white riesling with

3. A midmorning work break in Wolxheim

perhaps the alternative of a slightly chilled light Alsatian pinot noir, the region's sole red.

For the cheese course, we normally jumped outside of Alsace. (Alsatians, like *les Français*, insist on red wine and strong cheese, and consider their pinot noir too light to stand up to the task.) At our inaugural Christmastime dinner together, Daniel uncorked one of his last bottles from his stock of Château Angélus '64 kept in a hall closet. The wine was well past its prime. But Daniel's gesture of opening a bottle he'd kept for decades was far greater than anything that could have been poured in the glass.

For dessert, usually a traditional pastry loaded with either cream or chocolate, he might open a bottle of sweet Alsace muscat, or if he were really feeling festive, an Alsatian *vendanges tardives*, a family of sweet concentrated white wines made from overripe "late harvest" grapes.

I became intrigued with the idea of joining *les vendanges* (the wine harvest) in the fall of 2003 after Daniel returned from Alsace bronzed and fit. He showed pictures of smiling men and women working in shorts and T-shirts and hoisting glasses in summerlike conditions in a gorgeous wine country of storybook villages and rolling vineyards at the foot of the Vosges Mountains.

Why not, I thought, do as Daniel and other Frenchmen do in the fall—take a vacation from computers and telephones and modernity to experience the *real* wine life in the provincial world of *la France profonde*? There would be none of the Napa or Bordeaux trappings: no three-star dining, no thermal baths, no lazy bike rides through the vineyards in full fall color, no wine-tasting seminars. Just eight-hour days of backbreaking work and harvest camaraderie.

An outdoorsman, hunter, and mushroom forager, Daniel was an old hand of the vendanges. For years he worked the harvests as a *porteur*, or carrier—a job that involved having a tub strapped to one's back for hauling knee-buckling loads of grapes out of the vines. The days of human "grape mules" were practically over. More and more, machines were replacing human hands during the harvest. In the vineyards where the harvesting was still done by hand, porteurs were now replaced by small tractors; now everyone did what was once considered the job of women and the elderly—*coupeur*, or cutter.

Over that winter, Daniel and I discussed joining the harvest together at the small Wolxheim vineyard of Jean-Bernard Siebert, a friend for thirty years. Then, as the following fall approached, Daniel began to back off: he was getting too old for any kind of harvest . . . it was raining too much in Alsace . . . and surely this harvest would see awful weather. Maybe it was best to wait until the following fall.

I was getting impatient about the idea. And I didn't want to talk about it for another year. Maybe I would go anyway, I told Daniel one Sunday morning. Daniel called me later at home to say he'd changed his mind and would come along. We were set to ride together, but on the eve of our departure, there was a complication: Michelle's mother, living in her home in Alsace, had locked herself in the house and was refusing to let in anyone, even family members. Daniel would accompany me, but he and Michelle would be preoccupied with family business. For the most part, I would be on my own.

That Sunday morning, we set out—Daniel and Michelle in their car—crossing northwestern Italy, Switzerland, and a piece of Germany. It was night when we arrived on the main square of Daniel's hometown of Molsheim. At La Metzig, a gabled renaissance building constructed by the local butcher's guild almost five hundred years ago and now a restaurant, we ate *flammeküeche*, Alsace's signature thin-crusted tarts of onions, cream, and bacon, which an old Alsatian legionnaire turned chef in Texas once described to me as "hmmmm . . . Château Le-good-shit." These flammeküeche, washed down with the house riesling, were savory to the point of lifting the soul. Indeed, I was feeling something close to inspiration.

But then, I hadn't done any work yet.

On Monday morning Daniel picked me up at my hotel for our ten-minute commute by car. Alsace is relatively small as French wine-producing areas go—a narrow, 100-mile-long circuit of well-exposed hillsides prized for sparse rainfall and a long, cool growing season. Legend has it that Julius Caesar became a fan of Alsace wines during his conquest of easternmost Gaul. Today Alsatian wines are coveted by neighboring Belgians as well as the Germans, who fought over the place for centuries.

As for Wolxheim (population 870), its rieslings were favored by two of its nineteenth-century rulers from different sides of the Rhine: Napoleon I and Kaiser Wilhelm II. In the latter part of the nineteenth century and the early twentieth century, wine production was nearly wiped out by the outbreak of the phylloxera parasite and the scalping of vineyards by German artillery companies on the eve of World War I (which would return Alsace to France until the outbreak of the next great war).

We pulled up to Siebert's winery, an ancient Benedictine flour mill straddling the river canal that ran along the edge of town. It was 8:05 a.m., and we were late—the work van had just left with a crew to pick pinot noir. After we had a bit of friendly exchange with

Siebert—eyes bloodshot and cigarette in hand—one of the winery hands offered to drive us to the site of the morning's picking.

As we left the village, we entered a land of vine-covered hills in a cloak of full autumn. There were no big estates here: just small, open, unmarked plots of side-by-side vine rows. To an outsider it was impossible to tell where one producer's vines ended and another's began. We were let out at a spot where we found more than a dozen other pickers, a tractor trailer for loading grapes, and Siebert's dog, a squat, friendly, yellow mutt named Tokay. The harvest foreman, Dominique, a tall red-headed mustachioed man wearing a blue jumpsuit, issued me a pair of clippers (Daniel already had his own pair of sharpened clippers that he carried in a leather belt holster) and gave both of us plastic buckets. He assigned us our vine rows, and we set to work.

Two people generally worked each side of a vine row, with another pair working the opposite side of the same vines. The main idea was to clip the fist-size bunches of grapes from the vine without cutting off your fingers or those of the picker across from you. We then dropped the grapes in our buckets, and when the buckets were full, we passed them underneath the vines to a central row where a small tractor waited to take the grapes to a trailer parked in the road.

Someone recognized Daniel and called out that he was late for work, noting that perhaps he had spent too much time in the *midi*, the south. "*Attention*, this is not the *midi* here," the same male voice called out to me half-seriously. "Here when we work, we work, and when we stop we stop."

I followed the example of the others, moving up and down at odd angles to collect grape bunches. In Alsace tradition, vines are generally trained along top-of-head-high wires to maximize sun exposure. But on my first morning of picking, most of the grapes seemed to be growing in the most difficult places to pick—at waist level or hanging just a few inches off the ground.

"Watch the leaves," Dominique warned in French as he observed my bucket filling up with enough fall color to make one of those harvest window displays. Grape leaves, I learned, don't go into the making of wine. "Watch the fingers too," a male voice said on the other side of the vine. "We've already had two injured this week."

After a few minutes, my bucket was full, and I called out "seau" (bucket) and placed it—loaded with about twenty pounds of grapes— underneath the vine. A hand from the next row pulled it away, and a few seconds later an empty bucket, kicked like a soccer ball, came flying back my way.

I learned quickly to distinguish rotting grapes (not to be picked) from *pourriture noble*, the desirable "noble rot" or gray botrytis mold that sweetens and fortifies great wines like Sauternes. I fell into a clipping rhythm—left hand holds, right hand cuts. Left. Right. Left. Right. The pace picked up and my mind began to drift. There were a couple of episodes in which my brain signals rebelled: Left. Right. R——. Once, I nearly removed at least two fingertips from my left hand.

Then, a few buckets into the day, I felt my back start to seize up. I considered myself more fit than most forty-six-year-old males, but nothing I'd ever done before could quite prepare me for the numbing ache that seemed to crawl up from the ball of my right foot and nest deep in some nexus of muscle and nerve and flesh in my lower back.

I let out a groan—the first of several involuntary sounds of pain I would make that first day. The work week had just begun and I was considering my options: I could quit, walk back to town, and enjoy the Alsace wine route like a normal visitor. Or I could stick it out and not have that shame to live down.

"Ça va?" Daniel called out from a row or two away, asking if I was all right.

"Oui!" I lied.

After finishing the first vine row, there was just enough time to straighten up, bite into a cluster of black, thick-skinned grapes, and take a glance around at the sun-splashed rows of fall gold and red vines that led up to a golden statue of the Good Lord, hands outstretched, at the crest of a nearby hill. I said a small prayer. Then it was time to descend the slope and attack more vines.

As the morning wore on, the work picked up pace, and so did the chatter among the pickers. The first thing that struck me was that my fellow pickers were weaving in and out of two languages: French and an odd German dialect, which, I learned, was Alsatian. The second thing that impressed me was just how downright chipper these people were for a Monday morning. Florence, a mother in her forties who usually works in a bank, was enthusiastically describing in painstaking detail a recipe for an onion tart. Arnold, a retired geography teacher, was talking about his passion, local historical research. Frantz, a local jack-of-all-trades and a composer of waltzes, simply amused himself with the idea of an American picking pinot in their midst.

"You're a *real* American?" Frantz, bearded and in his late fifties, asked in French.

"The real Americans are on reservations," interjected Bernard, a vacationing security guard, from two vine rows away.

"Do they pick grapes by hand in California?" Frantz asked me.

I said that I thought California grapes were harvested mostly by migrant workers and machines.

"That's the U.S.A. *mécanisation*," Frantz said.

"*Stérilisation*," someone rhymed.

"*Purification*," Frantz continued, ". . . *pasteurisation* . . . *homogénisation*."

I was hurting, feeling out of place, and resigned to the fact that I might just become the object of ritual humiliation. After all, the U.S. presidential election was just weeks away, morning had just begun, and no one had yet even brought up the inevitable topic of George W. Bush and the Iraq war.

Then, suddenly, miraculously, the work came to a stop.

"Time for a drink!" Dominique called out.

It was 10:30 a.m. and everyone gathered around the tractor. Right there on the weather-beaten red hood of the Supertigre 7700, Dominique laid two rows of glass tumblers. Into these he first poured out small doses of red cassis syrup. Then he pulled the cork out of a wine bottle and filled the glasses to their brims with pinot blanc.

It would be the first of many morning cocktail breaks that week.

We saluted and drank. Cans of pâté and country terrines were opened. Butcher paper was unfurled, revealing two varieties of dried sausage that was cut up with pocket knives. Loaves of bread were passed around and torn up by hand. We devoured it all and drained our glasses.

"Ça va?" Daniel asked again, giving me a wary look.

At this point it became clear to me that in spite of the pain, and what California agricultural researchers call "high risk factors for musculoskeletal disorders (MSDs)," I was going to get by—the old-fashioned way.

"Ça va."

At noon we climbed into the panel van outfitted with benches made from wood planks and plastic crates and headed back to the winery for lunch. Siebert stood at the winery loading dock, watching as the trailer loaded with the morning's pickings tilted up and slowly dumped its contents into a small de-stemming machine. A hose connected to a pump spat the juice and skins into a nearby fiberglass vat where they would steep together a day or longer before being pressed.

The midday meal was prepared by Gérard, a chef on vacation from a local retirement home who took great pleasure in the ceremony of his job, wearing chef whites embroidered with his name and detailing the daily menu on a chalk board and easel by the entrance to the dining room. Actually, to call it a dining room is a stretch: it was a modest, multipurpose canteen-bar-kitchen-office area where we ate at a pair of long plywood tables covered with plastic table sheeting that bore the logo of Siebert's bank.

Siebert arrived with his crew from the wine cellar—a group of guys that included a local glass cutter and a retired motorcycle cop. He sat at the head of the table and stopped smoking just long enough to eat and tell some bawdy jokes with punch lines in Alsatian that made the men laugh and the women shake their heads.

That first day's lunch began with a plate including a slab of pâté surrounded by a trio of shredded vegetable salads. White wine was poured from bottles bearing no labels. When I asked what we were drinking, Siebert answered by saying it was a house blend of several varietals. He was cut off by one of my fellow pickers, a white-haired man with a thick mustache who suggested that Siebert should not divulge too much to me. After all, what would keep me from going to California and making Alsatian-style wine there? This was the first of three occasions on which someone would raise the suspicion that I could be an American spy.

For the main course, we ate family-style portions of grilled white sausages and fries. As I looked around the table, I was struck by the seeming equality in the group—the absence of any outward signs of social class or station. At first glance it would be almost impossible to tell the grape pickers from the proprietor in his disheveled jeans and sweatshirt. The workers, Alsatians who were working for French minimum wage (at the time about $9 an hour), were here because they wanted to be here.

I learned that Dominique, the head of our team, was an industrial engineer who worked for an enterprise that designed everything from airplane flaps to instruments to seismic labs to machinery for the nearby Bugatti automobile plant. He took more than a month of accumulated time off in the fall to pick grapes in Alsace and Burgundy and with his brother-in-law in Switzerland. "I like the nature, the ambience, *tout*," Dominique said, pouring another round.

After everyone helped themselves to seconds, platters of fruit and cheese were set out, including the local favorite, Munster, from the nearby village of the same name. For the finale, a liter bottle of transparent liquid was set on the table along with dainty stemmed shot glasses. "Mirabelle" was hand-scrawled on a small white label, indicating that the contents were yellow plum liquor, also known as "Le whiskey d'Alsace."

As both the new guy and, as far as anyone knew, the first American to pick grapes in Wolxheim, it was my duty to show my mettle. I felt all eyes on me as I lifted the delicate glass. I tilted my head back and drained it in one long swig that sent a warm glow up from stomach through my chest and up to the follicles on top of my head. More shots were passed around, followed by a box of cigars.

Then it was time to go back to labor.

That afternoon, work was in a vineyard known as Altenberg de Wolxheim, one of Alsace's fifty grand cru sites in a regional system of rating vineyard terroir that began only in the 1970s. An afternoon sun warmed the slopes; the pickers removed outer layers of sweatshirts and parkas. First we picked riesling—perfect golden ripe grapes growing in chalky soil. We ended the day nearby in rows of muscat—tiny, compact, sun-browned grape clusters. At the end of one vine row—fully facing the afternoon sun—I bit into a bunch of grapes.

The skins dissolved in my mouth and the juice that ran out was light and sweet and tasted like . . . muscat . . . sunshine . . . and meadow flowers impatient to be turned into wine.

That evening, after a long hot shower, I drove back to the winery to join Siebert, Dominique, and a small group for dinner in the same multipurpose room in the winery. I knew a few things about Siebert from Daniel: In the closed rural society of Wolxheim, he had been raised as a prince with a chauffeur and a nanny. Siebert's grandfather, Marcel, a local doctor, had been the first winemaker in the village to put wine in bottles. His father, Jean, whom Siebert referred to as "a monsieur," served in the French army and, like most men of his generation, was conscripted into the German army when Hitler decided to annex Alsace. "My father never talked about the war," Jean-Bernard would say. "Never." His father died young while Jean-Bernard was still in his twenties.

After a stint at a vintner's school in southern Alsace, Jean-Bernard took over the winery in the 1970s and began modernizing. He lived in the apartments upstairs from the winery. His mother lived in the house across the courtyard, and his brother Bruno, the mayor of Wolxheim and the head of a successful poultry processing company, lived on the same piece of property a few yards down the canal.

Though he was raised with privilege, Siebert disliked pretense. In spite of his background, he seemed to have succeeded in becoming a paysan. His wines were served in Michelin-starred restaurants and won gold and silver medals in European competitions, and yet his prices lagged behind many of his peers.

His Riesling de Wolxheim 2001, which won a gold medal in international competition, sold for exactly 6 euros and 10 centimes (about $8). His most expensive wine, a grand cru riesling made from Altenberg grapes, topped his price list at 6.70 euros, or less than $9 a bottle. This was at a time when some of his more ambitious contemporaries were winning international notice and selling their wines for five and ten times those prices. He seemed content to remain a typical small Alsatian producer with about sixteen acres of vines scattered around the hills of Wolxheim. He had a natural suspicion of both big estates that pumped out wine like refineries and the elite producers. "There are restaurants that sell Alsace wine for five, six euros a glass to tourists," Siebert told me that evening. "It's just not right." I didn't have the heart to tell him those were New York prices of twenty years ago.

Siebert, I would come to learn, was also going through a nasty divorce—one in which his ex-wife, who worked for years with Siebert in the winery, apparently felt that she was entitled to a share. Meantime, at fifty-one, he had a live-in female friend with whom he'd fathered a daughter, now more than a year old. Though I sat at the same table as Siebert and his companion, we were never introduced. Daniel and Michelle didn't even know the woman's name. Siebert's mother, when I spoke with her later that week, merely referred to the woman as "la nouvelle."

For starters that evening, we ate country pâtés served with light, sweet gewürztraminer. Joining us were a few of the guys who made up Siebert's winemaking crew. I had come to notice that Siebert ran his operation like a clubhouse where the wine, beer, and drinks were free all day. It was hard to tell who was working. Anyone, I noticed, could pour himself a drink—and often did—whenever he wanted. This usually started well before lunch and extended well into the night.

The dinner served by *la nouvelle* was roasted *pintade* (guinea fowl) served on a bed of lentils cooked with bacon and served with Siebert's pinot noir. After the meal and a few drink-inspired insults between the couple, Siebert's mate disappeared through the doorway leading up to the upstairs apartment, and left Siebert and a small group of men drinking Mirabelle. At one point, I'd asked Siebert about mechanical harvesting, which was being used more and more across France and the wine world as a fast and cheap alternative to hand picking.

Siebert explained that he tried mechanical harvesting on a small fraction of his fifteen acres of vines in 1998, "and it was . . . *pffft,*" he said making the sound of air being let out of a balloon. Machines can't pick between ripe and rotten grapes, and "the result was no good."

"Yes, I know they say they have improved the machines now, but I just don't believe in them," Siebert said. Oftentimes, when in thought, he would neglect his cigarette, letting it form long ashes that would tumble on the table or the floor.

"It's personal," he said. "I am anti-machine."

"One day the machines will do everything," he went on, "and that will be the day I stop drinking wine."

The next morning I awoke in a state of paralysis. My entire body, except for my hands, eyelids, lips, and toes, did not want to move. I rolled to the end of the bed, dropped my knees to the floor, and slowly raised myself upright.

Breakfast was coffee and ibuprofen.

"I remember the first day I did the *vendanges*—I was ready to cry," Florence, the bank worker, explained to me through the vines later that morning. "But every day is better." I hoped to hell she was right.

That day the ranks of pickers had dwindled by about three or four people. Daniel was off dealing with his mother-in-law and would be gone for the rest of the week. Frantz, perhaps astonished that I'd shown up again for more punishment, stopped referring to me as *l'Americain* and began calling me "Robess," my name in Alsatian. I was still the foreigner, I still couldn't make out half of what was being said, but I began to feel as if I belonged there.

A pair of Spanish brothers, one of whom spent evenings playing flamenco guitar in a restaurant in Strasbourg, were pummeling me with questions about America: *Is it true you can buy milk and cigarettes in Spanish there? Can you hunt sanglier* (wild boar) *there?*

At lunchtime we were joined by a man introduced to me as Antoine, a seventy-seven-year-old *tonnelier* (wine barrel maker) with fingers like sausages. His only lunch was a small cup of coffee and a shot of Mirabelle, and then he took to the vines with us.

That afternoon was memorable because the work was a grueling hill of riesling more than a hundred yards long that finished with a particularly steep ascent. The grape clusters in this well-exposed slope were fat and healthy and the going was slow. Rain from the night before had dampened the ground just enough for mud to stick to our rubber boots and gradually grow into large, heavy clods.

Toward the top of the hill, the pickers fell silent. There were just the cries of "seau, seau," grunts, and other bodily noises and—about a hundred yards away—you could hear the whine of a mechanical harvesting machine that could do our work in a matter of minutes. After we reached the top, we descended and did it all over again on some adjacent rows.

Maybe it was exhaustion or delirium, but what pushed me forward was the illusion that we were somehow working to preserve a bit of humanity among the vines—this group of people who came together and shared their lives and their ills and their dreams.

Could there be something oddly subversive in manual labor? Or was this simply the effect of drinking pinot blanc since breakfast?

As we reached the top of the hill for the second time, I straightened up and looked out over a brilliant landscape; the cloud cover had dispersed, and the sky was a brilliant blue.

Having survived that afternoon, I felt stronger and seemed to stand straighter. Back at the winery, I spoke with Siebert, who looked tired and appeared to have slept in his clothes from the night before. He stood, unshaven, among his stainless steel fermenting tanks. There was the usual hum of activity: hoses, pumps, centrifuges, tanks, and a handful of guys—some working, some watching, some drinking.

Siebert offered me a glass and we walked among his fermenting tanks, tasting juice at its beginning stages of turning to wine. It was yeasty and sweet and fizzy with carbonic gas—like the muscat I'd picked a day earlier but with the promise of another dimension that pricked the tongue.

This year, Siebert said, would be *moyenne*. Although the word literally means "average," in daily French it generally connotes something worse than that. The vines had been smeared by mildew; Siebert had been late in removing leaves and had to sulfur-treat the vines more than he would have wished. "But you know what, I don't decide that." Siebert pointed the overly long tip of his cigarette heavenward and said, "He does."

Siebert then opened up one small steel vat of a couple of hundred liters—many times smaller than most of his steel tanks. He motioned me onto a step so I could stick my head in the vat and smell the wine. He then drew a glass from a metal faucet. It was tokay pinot gris, far more floral and complex than Siebert's usual stuff. "It's my personal stock," Siebert said. "From a few special vines."

I wondered if Siebert was capable of a great signature wine, and if in fact he was not making it—for him and his pals. I mentioned to Siebert the name of a producer in the upper Rhine who was winning international accolades and whose wines were selling at prices that matched those of Bordeaux *crus classées*. Siebert gave me a blank look and rolled his eyes. I asked Siebert why he was uninterested in selling his wines for more.

"You know why? You know what I would have?" Siebert asked. "One day they will put me in a two-meter hole and people will come and shed two or three tears and what good would the money be then?"

"This," Siebert said, waving around him at the tractors, the people, and the vats of fermenting wine. "This is what I do it for. This is my life."

Madame Yvonne Siebert, Jean-Bernard's mother, was a stately, well-coiffed woman who maintained a bourgeois existence across the courtyard from her bohemian winemaking son. I had expressed an interest in the history of the property, and one day she gave me a tour of her house, showing me the room full of her late husband's hunting trophies as well as her kitchen display of metal and ceramic tableware used by the mill's Benedictine inhabitants five centuries earlier. Then we sat in the dining room—lined with thick, rich wood paneling and wonderfully ornate wood hutches. Jesus suffered on a cross on top of her stereo system in the corner.

Madame Siebert went rummaging around in a closet to pull out some old family documents and mementos of the mill. There were pictures in boxes and centuries-old documents in books. But what I remember most is what followed. Mrs. Siebert pushed all of it aside and began to tell me about her son and some of the uglier elements of his divorce, including the fact that she had not been able to see her grandchildren.

"Do you have any idea what that is like, monsieur?" Her eyes welled up with tears. "Jean-Bernard is too good. He doesn't care about business, just making good wine," she said. "I worry so much about him. You see how he smokes like a chimney. And I know there are profiteers who come and drink at his table and listen like this"—she touched her elbows on the table—"and they go and tell everything to his ex."

"And now," she went on, "he's gone off and had a baby with *la nouvelle* . . . I just don't understand. I don't understand how things are nowadays . . . But you didn't come to talk about that . . . Where were we, monsieur?"

My final morning of the work week, I arose from bed—miraculously—without pain and without requiring medication.

My last hours of work were particularly difficult. That afternoon we attacked a long, steep ascent of about two hundred yards of pinot blanc. Then it began to rain. I had left my rain parka in the truck several hundred yards from where we were working, and my sweatshirt became heavy with water. Marguerite, the retired schoolteacher, offered me her plastic parka.

"No," I said.

"Oui," she said, insisting that her canvas jacket underneath was sufficient. She turned a corner at her waist inside out. "See, it's waterproof."

The rain turned into downpour. I took the parka and continued working. Here was a woman a quarter century my senior cheerfully insisting that I needed her raincoat more than she did. I was, frankly, humbled.

We worked without break for three hours, tired, toting boulders of mud on our rubber boots, and straining as each water-sopped bucket grew heavier than the last. As we finished work that afternoon, the rain stopped. Fog blanketed the floor of the valley below, and the sun broke though the clouds above.

The week I had spent here was one of the strangest of my life. It was stoop labor a long way from home with co-workers who reverted to a tongue I couldn't begin to decipher. Yet rarely have I so quickly felt so close to a place and a group of people.

If wine is a reflection of the winemaker, then the wine made from these grapes would surely bear the marks of the chaos that was Siebert—standing there casually crediting the Almighty with his cigarette ash.

After returning to the winery, I was saying my goodbyes to the team members when I felt myself lifted up high by several hands from behind. I flew up to the lip of a trailer of grapes and was dumped in face first. The juice went everywhere—burning my eyes and sticking to my skin.

Baptism by grapes is a tradition here. I can now say it changes a man. Up to the moment I met a few tons of pinot face first, I held to the thought of wine as a sort of mysterious potion made by experts or magicians. In Wolxheim I saw wine as part of a cycle of life—as natural as childbirth and death—made from some of the last fruit of the year picked and fermented with human sweat, blood, and spirit. Raising a glass could never be the same.

Among the Mayonnaise

THREE

WHAT FIRST BROUGHT ME TO LES MAYONS was not the call of
the vines, but the frogs. Nestled among the Maures, the sprawling
range of low, dark, forested mountains of the central Var, and just
off the hairpin route that leads to St. Tropez, Les Mayons is a typical
Provençale village—neither chic nor touristy nor, mercifully, very
developed. The village is home to about five hundred people, with
its one bakery, one *epicerie/tabac* (grocery/tobacconist) that serves
as a general store, one jam maker, and one bar that is headquarters
to a local *pétanque* club: La Boule Mayonnaise.

Les Mayons lies in the heart of what I have come to know as one
of the most hidden yet rewarding corners of southern France. Below
the town is a gently rolling landscape: stands of cork oaks and pine
meet Provençal jungle, fields of wildflowers, bee keepers, shepherds
and vineyards. Atop a nearby mountain peak at the end of a road
to nowhere, the chapel of Notre Dames des Anges is cared for by
a couple of Filipino monks; suspended from the chapel rafters is a
giant crocodile.

We arrived *en famille*—my wife and I with our then eight-year-
old son—after dusk in early spring 2003 for an environmental
outing led by a group of French scientists and naturalists who
called themselves Operation Frequence Grenouille (Operation Frog
Proliferation), an organization dedicated to the preservation and
well-being of the tailless order of amphibians classified as Anura.
In other words, frogs and toads.

This evening started in a small room with peeling walls in the Les
Mayons city hall. The leader of the frog lovers—a stout toad of a

4. Claude Martin at his winery

man with a thick black beard and decked out in dark camouflage—
showed us slides of various local amphibious species accompanied
by recordings of their mating calls, which can sound like squawking
chickens or the clacking of *pétanque* balls.

Up to this point, my most intimate experience with frogs had
been the odd encounter on the dinner plate. This evening, however,
there would be no frog legs sautéed in Pouilly-Fuissé, nor even
a local white Côtes-de-Provence. Commercial frog hunting and

ranching have been prohibited in France for decades, ever since the French government realized the passion for frog thighs had led to an uncomfortable spike in the mosquito population. As a result, now the frog legs served in Paris bistros are invariably shipped in frozen from Asia.

Monsieur Toad railed against some of the dangers facing the contemporary frog: from real estate development intruding on frog habitats to moms who dump the family goldfish in a local pond. (Fish eat frog eggs, and frogs by instinct apparently avoid laying eggs in places that would put their family tree at risk of being devoured as fish food.)

After the lecture portion of the program, we suited up in rubber boots and headlamps and headed out to the marshes around Les Mayons to track down the first frogs of spring at the beginning of their mating season. A silvery near-full moon lit the floor of the plain. Everywhere, it seemed, there were sounds to track among the tall grasses. And that we did—a group of more than a dozen adults and children—searching out frogs and shining our lights and video cameras on them as they courted or coupled in the mud.

By the time our romp in the swamps wound down about midnight, I'd added one more species to my very short "don't eat" list.

What sent me back to Les Mayons was a guy in a loud silk shirt. I was eating lunch at a sidewalk table in Lorgues, a small but bustling town in the Var. I was listening to the pair of guys next to me hold forth on food and wine. After more or less inserting myself into their conversation, I learned that Olivier, the guy in the loud shirt, was a building contractor from Draguignan who was not shy about expressing his opinions.

In this part of the Var, the biggest name in cuisine is Bruno, the renowned over-the-top truffle king, who serves multicourse truffle orgies from his overdecorated old farmhouse with the jet-set helicopter pad. "Bruno's head is like this now," Olivier said, holding up two big meaty hands at a distance of nearly a meter. "It's not a restaurant anymore. It's a restaurant of the stars." To add the final touch of proof for his argument, Olivier brought up Bruno's association with France's notorious aging glitter-suited rocker. "Johnny Halliday is his friend," he said with a dismissive wave of the hand.

When I told Olivier of the nearby winery that I planned to visit that afternoon for an article I was writing on the Côtes-de-Provence region he protested, Olivier warned me that it had met a similar fate as Bruno's place. "That's not a winery anymore!" Again the dismissive wave. "It's become a vacation village!"

I went by the place anyway. Olivier was right. This once reputed winery and vineyard that called itself a "château" had been transformed into something resembling a Disney resort with restaurants, a cooking school, a hotel, a swimming pool, golf, and a gift shop selling the château's golf shirts and knickknacks. And worst of all, you had to pay to taste the wine. The promotional literature announced "guided visits" for a fee of ten euros: "After a short tour of La Cave, discover one of our two Cuvées in the company of a professional who will teach you to appreciate the charms of wines from the Côtes-de-Provence." I got out of there in a hurry.

I later tasted this wine on occasion in restaurants, and without the benefit of a professional who could teach me to appreciate its particular charms . . . I found it drinkable but unmemorable.

"Now, if you're looking for something original . . . ," Olivier had said, "there is a guy who is making some interesting *vin de pays* in Les Mayons."

Olivier had said the right words. One morning the following week, my wife and I set out for Domaine Borrely-Martin. We pulled up the dirt road through the rows of just-budding vines and arrived at a small farmhouse. We were greeted by barking dogs, and then by Claude Martin. Martin, who wore a graying ponytail, grey-flecked facial stubble, and an expression free of any apparent stress, said he hadn't been expecting anybody. That morning a water line had burst, he added, pointing to a muddy hole in the ground with exposed pipe.

Metal and fiberglass winemaking vats sat outside under a tiled carport structure. No fancy winemaking apparatus here: I was sure there was no resort community here, no gift shop, nor a wine professional who would teach me to appreciate the charms of the wines.

I offered to Martin that we would come back some other time. He thought about it a few seconds, considered the muddy hole, and then waved us toward the house. The plumbing could wait. He directed us to a small wood table and chairs in the grass next to a makeshift pen holding one sheep that seemed to be somewhere between the size of a lamb and an adult ewe. Also next to the table and tied between two trees was a clothesline with the family laundry.

Martin went to root around in his "cellar"—a stone, air-conditioned garage that I later saw was crammed with bottles from floor to ceiling. He emerged with the first bottle: a 1998 that was dominated by carignan grapes. The wine was deeply colored, packed with explosive fruit and earth, and, it seemed, contained a much higher degree of alcohol than the 13 percent Martin claimed. Then out came a second, a 1999 of 100 percent mourvèdre—the grape that dominates the concentrated leathery wines of the Bandol coast about an hour southwest of Les Mayons. This mourvèdre had raging tannins that made our gums itch and our lips pucker. A third followed—another '99, this one a blend of syrah and grenache that he called Le Carré de Laure—which seemed to have it all: the fruit, the tannins, the earth, the alcohol kick. All three were so different and yet tasted like nothing I'd ever before experienced. These were wines with strong individual personalities and substance that coated your tongue and left a layer of sediment in the bottle as thick as Turkish coffee. They were simultaneously rustic and beautifully seductive.

Martin pulled a packet of Pall Mall tobacco out of his shirt pocket along with some rolling paper. After pouring some of the tobacco into the paper, he neatly rolled a cigarette with one hand, licked it, and poised it between his index and middle fingers. He put away the tobacco and produced a plastic lighter, firing up the end of his cigarette.

Then forty, Martin explained that he was a onetime sports journalist who had given up writing less than a decade earlier to work the vines on this property that has been in his family—the Borrely side of his mother—more than two and half centuries. What he operated chiefly with the help of his wife, Olivia, and his brother Jacques, who works weekdays as a tax department bureaucrat in Nice, was not so much a winery as a wine laboratory. While he sold the harvest of most of his land—about thirty-four acres—to the local wine cooperative, he reserved another twelve acres for production of his own vin de pays, local wine a step above table wine, which he sells through wine and food fairs, restaurants in and around St. Tropez, and out of his garage.

While Martin's operation wasn't technically *biologique* (organic), he explained, he used no pesticides (forbidden in this area because it serves as a sanctuary on a bird migration route) or herbicides or chemical fertilizers. While he used no wood in the aging of wines, Martin did often wait an extraordinary amount of time—years, in fact, before he felt his reds were worthy of release. Martin said he had chosen to market his wine as vin de pays des Maures and shunned the Côtes-de-Provence label—because the appellation was now too crowded with high-dollar winemakers for him to compete effectively.

Martin then went back into his garage and emerged with another bottle, his 2000 Le Carré de Laure dominated by cabernet sauvignon. The fact that Martin felt free enough to radically change the mix of what went into a particularly branded wine was both astounding and refreshing. On the one hand, his cab-today-gone-tomorrow attitude defied some basic ideas of labeling. Yet Martin explained that he was not interested in making his wines taste the same from year to year, but in making the best wines he could from any given year's crop. And like a musician following an elusive muse, Martin's idea of what was best in any year was based upon what he found personally inspiring at the time.

Martin poured some of this bottle, and it tasted like what I expected from a cabernet blend, starting with the solid structure and the bold fruit. After the other wines, there was something *normal* about it, referential, and I said so.

"Ah, but it's an Anglo-Saxon reference," Martin answered with the intellectual one-upmanship of a French TV talk-show guest. He again conducted the tobacco ritual with his Pall Mall pouch, papers, and the lighter, while continuing, "Cabernet has nothing to do with Provence."

In my adult life I'd drunk more bottles of wine than I could count. Yet up until this point, a couple of years into my living in France, I'd never really understood that wine grapes could be so charged with history and baggage. Anglo-Saxon? Indeed, it was Eleanor of Aquitaine's marriage to England's Henry II in the mid-twelfth century that left a lasting English mark on Bordeaux and later fueled a century of war. Cabernet and merlot are Bordeaux. And Bordeaux by virtue of its geopolitical position established its wines as the gold standard of the English-speaking world.

All I cared about at that moment was what was in my glass, and with every glass there was a new surprise. Martin's wines were simply *different* from anything I'd experienced. They were off the grid of my preconceptions. In short, this was the first time I'd really *tasted* wine. That afternoon opened up a new world for me that I've never left—or wanted to leave.

More bottles appeared. The sheep rubbed against the posts of her pen and studied us like a curious toddler in her playpen. After about an hour and a half of this, I brought up the subject of buying wine. Oh no, Martin complained, he couldn't possibly *sell* us wine on such short notice. He stored the bottles without labels and capsules, which would have to be put on. Then the wine would have to be boxed. Besides, it was now lunchtime. Could we come back, he asked, maybe next week?

I did come back again and again: I loved sharing Martin's quirky, original wines with friends, and as I got to know Martin better, I enjoyed being around a winemaker who was just as original.

The following spring we returned to Les Mayons, with some trepidation. The hot and dry summer of 2003 brought forest fires— set by the annual parade of pyromania—that burned thousands of acres in the Var, including the Maures. As it turned out, the flames had stopped about three and half miles from Les Mayons.

At Borrely-Martin there was now a small stone and outbuilding the size of a tool shed, with a small tiled terrace—Martin explained he was building an office and tasting room. The sheep was nowhere in sight. The clothesline was gone. Nothing else seemed to have changed. Martin still wore a few days worth of stubble and his perpetual look of calm.

Once he started talking in his sort of rapid-fire monotone, he barely came up for air. An American importer had found him and had begun distributing some of his wines in Virginia. The problem was that, once the cost of middlemen and shipping was added to his wines, the costs were nearly doubled, putting the price of his wines at around $20—more than all but the most iconoclastic Americans were willing to spend on an unknown wine.

Robert Parker's *Wine Advocate* had favorably reviewed two of his wines: his standard vin de pays ("This rustic wine has outstanding depth of fruit . . . and is loaded with cigar, balsam, juniper berry as well as blackcurrant flavors") and his 2000 Anglo-Saxonized Le Carré de Laure ("a powerful yet graceful feminine wine"). Following that, a large U.S. importer had inquired about representing Martin's wines—provided, of course, that Martin could guarantee "no interruption of stock." "How could I do that?" Martin asked quizzically. "I only have so many bottles, and then what would I sell to people who come by here to buy wine?"

Martin went on with typically French fatalism, a state of mind in which the glass can never be half full because of a very long and complicated list of reasons—chief among them the fact that if there is half a glass remaining, it will surely get drunk, and then what? The sick French economy, the cost of basic food and staples, he complained, along with the government's crackdown on drinking and driving, was killing the good life. Wine sales were depressed; people weren't going out as much or entertaining. "The French are very tight right now," Martin observed, rolling the first of many cigarettes that afternoon. "It's everyone for himself. It's a true crisis." Then Martin lit his cigarette and asked if maybe we should start with white wine that afternoon. The sky was gray; there was a humid chill in the air.

Martin's white was a light limpid 2003 made from forty-year-old clairette vines. Clairette is known as a fragile grape that has fallen out of favor because it's thought to not age or travel well. From the first sniff, Martin's clairette smelled of wildflowers. It was light, uncomplicated—a simple glass of springtime.

Next, it was on to rosé, a wine that Martin said he did not enjoy making. "I make rosé because that's what people want, what they expect here in Provence," Martin offered. "The people who like my rosé are the people who normally don't like rosé." Martin's rosé was pure mourvèdre, and was more than a few shades darker than the pale rose-petal or salmon rose–kissed tones sold by the tanker along the Côte d'Azur. The result was a bit schizophrenic: it had some of the heat of a muscular red followed by the citrus feel of a traditional rosé. "I don't know," Martin commented. "It's not red, it's not white . . ." Martin sipped, spat the wine out in the dirt next to some vines, and tossed the rest of the glass after it. "It doesn't interest me."

Then Martin brought out a succession of reds. Olivia, a woman with strong, sharp features and long jet-black hair, joined us for a couple of glasses, rolled and smoked a cigarette, and quietly went back to the house. Martin's mood remained on the somber end of his seemingly flat mood scale as he turned introspective, philosophical.

How is it, he wondered, that bigger vineyards around him could produce such uninteresting wines and sell them at such elevated prices? Or why, for example, would someone spend $50 for a bottle of wine from Argentina? At one point, Martin let out that he had begun teaching winemaking part-time at the local agricultural high school to make ends meet for his family, which included two daughters: Lea, in middle school, and Victoria, a toddler.

"I think when people buy wine from someone, they are buying a piece of the man," he said, finishing off the very small end of his thin, unfiltered cigarette. "They are buying a story, and I think they prefer if the winemaker has at least as much money as they do—or more."

I started to protest, but Martin wasn't listening.

"For example, most people, if they bought a property like this, would turn the house into a palace, they'd put in a French garden and swimming pool and park a Porsche out front," Martin went on. "And when the people buy wine from someone like that, they pay for the swimming pool, the garden, the Porsche, but that's okay with them because it's the story they're buying."

"I think they come here and the first thing they notice is: there is no cash."

By the time we had finished drinking, the clouds had dissipated and a low, luminous evening sun—the kind that in this part of the world often comes out at the end of an otherwise colorless afternoon—lit up the rows of trimmed vines showing their first leaves. At this moment looking out over Martin's land, it was evident just how rich he was.

"Yes," he said, "this is my sanctuary, but I don't know that it will last. People in the village are already tearing up their vines to build houses," he said. "My goal is to hold on as long as possible. I would have to reach an extreme state of poverty before I would sell."

In the years since that conversation, I've returned to Borrely-Martin countless times. And every time after I leave the A8 Motorway and wind to Les Mayons through stands of cork oaks and pines, the sheepherders and bee farms and frog swamps, and the gently sloping vineyards planted in reddish clay, below the looming mountains, I think, *This is how man was meant to live*. And as I turn up the washed-out road that leads to the domain, I feel as though I am visiting an old, yet unpredictable, friend.

On one of those trips in the fall of 2005, I was received by Olivia, who was in bright spirits. Business was good. Borrely-Martin wines had won a succession of praise in French wine journals, and his Le Carré de Laure 2001 had won the highest rating in the French wine bible, the Guide Hachette. A faithful and growing clientele of wine lovers—Germans, English, Swedes, and Americans—was making its way to Les Mayons. Some wines were now selling as Côtes-de-Provence. The tasting room now had glass shelves displaying bottles and honors and even a spittoon. Wines were packed, ready to buy in cases. There was even, next to the computer in the corner, a credit card machine.

This time I asked about the lamb. Olivia explained how the project to raise one domestic ewe ended sadly when the animal grew forlorn in her solitariness and at times aggressive around small children. They gave her to a local shepherd, but she had become too domesticated to fit in with a herd . . . and, Olivia said with a sad shake or her head and black hair, she was killed. Now the Martins allowed the shepherd to graze hundreds of sheep in their vines in winter, providing a natural source of weed control and fertilizer.

I noticed new stainless steel vats packed tightly under what seemed a growing open-air structure in front of the Martin home, as well as a hydraulic press parked outside in the elements. At the other end of the house was a fiberglass above-ground swimming pool. Her husband still worked as a part-time schoolteacher. There was still no excess of cash, but, at least, she said, "We are organized now."

The following year, when I told Martin that a friend and I were interested in making our own wine in my garage, he invited us to come pick grapes from his vineyard. I figured that he wanted us to buy his grapes, but in fact he turned down any recompense, turning us loose in the vines.

The picking took place on a warm September morning. Joining me were two fellow Americans—my partner in home winemaking, Ken McNeill, who worked days making software systems for satellites, and his wife, Joyce, a urologist, who often spent her nights in surgery in French public hospitals. Martin directed us to a few vine rows of tight, perfect clusters of young syrah. He showed us how to test for ripeness by gently squeezing the grapes between the forefinger and thumb to feel the elastic skin of the grape, and he insisted that we stack each bunch neatly with the others as if we were collecting table grapes for a banquet. In the weeks and months that followed he generously and patiently tutored us every step of the way—lending me whatever equipment I might need, indulging my most basic questions about turning grapes to wine, and tasting and fretting with us over the course of months as our baby syrah developed.

One of the surprising things about Martin was just how classically French this wine hippie could be. Without giving it much thought, I had addressed Martin for years with the formal *vous*. Martin politely asked one day if I would be bothered conversing in the familiar *tu* form.

Another thing is, Claude Martin doesn't really fret. He was, however, very *present* in almost every moment I spent with him during that time. That is to say, while I fretted over each stage of our crude winemaking operation and sought "what do we do now?" answers, Martin remained cool, deadpan, yet at the same engaged—providing instruction that was intuitive and sometimes enigmatic.

After we fermented the wine in a large plastic food container, I asked Martin how long we should let it macerate with its skins and seeds before pressing. Well, Martin explained, that was difficult to say. We needed to taste it daily. First the wine would become more and more tannic, and it would reach the point where it was almost hard to stand. Then, just as we thought the wine was undrinkable, it would begin to mellow, to round out. At the moment we found it pleasing—we should let the wine flow out and press the skins. For now, Martin was adamant, we needed *surtout* (above all) to keep air out of the container: since we didn't yet have the sort of floating airtight lid we needed to do the job, we'd have to improvise. Carbon dioxide is often used in wineries big and small to blow oxygen out of vats and seal them from air. Martin hoisted a large CO_2 tank into the trunk of my car with a "Here, take this, but I need it back."

Once the wine had been pressed and siphoned into another vat, Professor Martin counseled us in the unpredictable secondary stage of malolactic fermentation in which bacteria convert the wine acids to lactic acid, softening its edges. Although do-it-yourself wine manuals counseled adding special cultures to force the fermentation, Martin counseled us to wait and let it occur spontaneously.

And how would we know that was happening? Of course we would do chemical tests and chromatography, but Martin was insistent that we should use the time-honored methods of sniffing and sipping. "I use the lab less and less," he said. "I depend more on my taste."

"You know that malo has started," he said, "when the wine smells like fresh goat cheese." I tasted the wine and tasted it. Was I smelling goat cheese? My neighbor's goats? Was it a memory of the cheese I had for lunch? Or was my mind playing tricks on me?

"*Ne t'inquiète pas*," Martin said over and over, telling me not to worry. "We are all more or less in the same boat when it comes to these things. No two vats are ever the same." Martin also taught me something else that I have learned to be true: No wine ever tastes the same. It changes week to week, day to day, glass to glass.

Often I'd arrive at Martin's place early in the morning. I'd walk around the back of his house and usually find Martin in the kitchen that had been hand painted by Olivia in bright colors with a high plank of wood that served as a bar. Across the room from the kitchen was a seating area with a raised open fireplace that was often lit on those cold autumn mornings. Martin, unshaven and energized by his first cups of coffee, would typically stand, pace in a pair of yellow Converse high-tops, and roll and ignite those little hand-rolled jobs that seemed to contain only about five puffs—just enough to push Martin's thoughts into another gear—before they were done.

Though I'd bring samples and come for advice on winemaking, our conversations rarely started with wine. One day it might be Mexican faith healing, another, modern painting. After a couple of cups of stovetop coffee, we would leave the kitchen and usually taste a variety of Martin's wines at all stages. Sometimes he would have me press my ear up against his vats to listen to the wine.

One day in mid-October, I found Martin in his kitchen with sheet music spread over the bar. This was in the middle of the fermenting season but Martin had other things on his mind. Laying on a couch nearby was an electric bass. Music, he explained, had been keeping him up late at night. Martin said that over the summer he had met a musician who had shared something with him that was nothing short of revelation. What had been revealed was this: that the beats of music are not fixed in time—that is, they can be slowed or quickened. Yet—and this was the essential thing—the end of every measure must be timed perfectly. "That is to say," Martin said as he paused from rolling a cigarette, "there is tremendous freedom, but in a perfect structure." As a result of this illumination, Martin had asked the man to reteach him the guitar—from the start.

Martin explained that a perfect example of this approach was his personal god. In this case, Martin was referring not to the Almighty, but—he said grinning—Eric Clapton, a master of improvisation. "In fact, it's like wine," Martin ventured. Like the great Clapton, Martin was striving within the structure of traditional winemaking to hit the divine notes that had never been played quite that way before.

Martin lit his cigarette, still standing in front of the counter, and he grew more intense. He went from Clapton's early career with Cream to Leonardo's divine proportions to the meticulously planned measures of the planners of the old cathedrals of Europe, to the geometry and optical illusions in Le Notre's first masterpiece—the gardens of the Château de Vaux le Vicomte. He drowned the stub of what remained of his cigarette in the sink and threw it away. He took a pencil and sketched directly on the bar to emphasize his point. And finally he spoke of the great vineyards, Cheval Blanc, Clos de Vougeot, Coulée de Serrant. Everything had been laid out a certain way for a reason—for multiple reasons. "Nothing," Martin said, setting his hands flat on the bar, "was done *n'importe quoi.*"

Martin had in those few words managed to crystallize the essence of fine winemaking and its balance of anarchy and order, of science and art, of doing and knowing when to leave well enough alone. Of resisting, certainly, the lax shrug that nowadays translates as "whatever."

FOUR

The Madman of Bandol

DEFINING WHERE THE FRENCH RIVIERA begins is easy; pin-pointing where it ends is almost impossible. The Riviera, or Côte d'Azur, starts in the east at the Italian border and stretches through the playgrounds of Monaco, the pebble beaches of Nice, and the palatial hotels of Cannes. The western frontier, however, is as murky as bouillabaisse: somewhere along a band of hundreds of kilometers that takes in the rugged red cliffs known as the Esterel, the hedonistic beach clubs of Saint Tropez, and the *calanques*, the famous rocky inlets before Marseille.

The Côte d'Azur defies mapmaking because it's a mind-set, a lifestyle. It's months-long traffic jams of fast cars going nowhere, impossibly sized yachts, miles of side-by-side beach lounges for rent, and plates of fish that cost an average day's wages. The wine that accompanies this cliché is usually rosé, usually bearing the lightest rose-petal blush, that when chilled and reflecting the midday Mediterranean light leads those who drink it to believe they are sipping nectar of the gods.

The seafront of Saint-Cyr-sur-Mer, on the road between Toulon and Marseille, has avoided annexation into that world. I first visited the beachfront of Saint-Cyr on a sunny day in May—a time when *le tout cinema* puts on a show known as the Cannes Film Festival with red carpets and private boats the size of aircraft carriers and when much of Europe flocks to the Riviera for long holiday weekends. On this day Saint-Cyr's beachfront was barely awake. A modest walkway and a small port look onto a yawning bay known as the Golfe d'Amour. The French Romantic poet and statesman Alphonse

5. Cyrille Portalis

Marie Louis de Lamartine—visiting here some two hundreds years ago—compared what he saw to the Bay of Naples.

To the east are miles of sandy coastline and tree-covered hills. To the west is the city of Ciotat and views of a pair of close-in islands: the Île Verte (Green Island) and the Bec de l'Aigle (Eagle's Beak), a jagged, vertical red rock defying the surf and the wind. Some say it is the distance from big cities and the rugged terrain that have kept development in check. Others say it's the wind—the mistral that rips down through the hills around Toulon and can make a missile out of anything that's not bolted down or turn a day at the beach into a sandstorm out of *Lawrence of Arabia*.

Whatever the reason, Saint-Cyr has remained happily pedestrian. The seafront restaurants with their terraces of plastic tables and bright-colored parasols serve *moules frites* (mussels with fries) and octopus salad and fried squid with rosé, which seems to pour out of bar faucets into carafes but when the sun is shining does the same sort of alchemical magic as the expensive stuff.

The young wear only enough to accessorize their tattoos. Elderly couples up from Marseille sport jaunty beach outfits—the men displaying jungles of white chest hair and gold chains. Yet the feel of the place is utterly unselfconscious un-Saint *Trop*, the anti-Cannes. The language spoken here is a saucy Pagnolesque Provençale that mocks all pretenses.

Saint-Cyr is important to the wine world because it is part of the Bandol wine appellation, spreading over three thousand acres around eight towns near the port of Bandol, which has exported wines since antiquity. Bandol is synonymous with mourvèdre, an uncommon and temperamental grape variety imported from Spain sometime in the Middle Ages that has made a comeback. After the phylloxera outbreak ruined the vineyards in 1870, the area was replanted with highly productive hybrids that were pressed into thin, mediocre table wine. It wasn't until the founding of the Bandol appellation in 1941 and the end of World War II that winemakers started replanting mourvèdre, which grows in tight grape clusters, susceptible to rot in wetter, less windy places. In Bandol, mourvèdre produces what are arguably the most robust, complex wines of Mediterranean coastal France: rich, spicy dry red wines and rosés that can even stand up to a rainy day.

Saint-Cyr is also significant because it is home to Château Pradeaux and winemaker Cyrille Portalis, who is known among his local peers as a *fou*, a "madman." On that first spring day visit to Saint-Cyr, I had arranged to meet Portalis, who is inheritor of the farm-estate that once belonged to the Count Jean-Marie-Étienne Portalis, known in French history books as the Napoleonic minister who coauthored the emperor's civil code and wrote the 1801 *Concordat*, reestablishing the role of the Catholic Church for the subsequent century. The main square of the village of Saint-Cyr, shaded by plane trees and graced by a gilded replica of the Statue of Liberty, is named Place Portalis after another ancestor who became mayor in 1860.

Cyrille Portalis is called crazy because he is insanely perfectionistic when it comes to making wine, which in the case of Pradeaux's reds means dense, leathery wine that can be rude in its youth but can last for decades.

Château Pradeux is located between the village and the sea, at the edge of housing developments that have slowly eaten away at the countryside and crept into the vines. I arrived through the side entrance on a bumpy dirt road barely wide enough for one compact car, and drove about forty yards through an iron arbor covered with climbing roses with treelike trunks that predated the French Revolution.

The "château" is a cracking old farmhouse—stone and gray masonry with bright green shutters—that shelters a small courtyard paved with a now-warped floor of irregular *galets*, or river stones, sprouting a fine carpet of weeds. This was clearly not one of those magazine-perfect renovations in Provence but a farm that seemed still inhabited by its ghosts and their living offspring.

I waited for Portalis in a cramped, low-ceilinged tasting room off the courtyard, where I was greeted by a sunny young woman who worked part-time helping Madame Portalis with the château administration and odd jobs. Mademoiselle made reference to Monsieur Portalis's perfectionism, saying, "He does everything relating to the wine . . . *Everything*." I was expecting a very serious gentleman farmer—a modern, countrified version of his famous ancestor, depicted in First Empire portraits with intense eyes, a high forehead and powdered wig, and aggressively angular cheekbones.

Madame Portalis walked through the door, dark-haired and matronly in a long skirt, accompanied by a man who appeared to be covered head-to-toe in dust, wearing old gym shorts, field-eaten boat shoes, and a faded T-shirt. I shook hands with her and then the man, who almost timidly reached out one labor-stained hand. It took a few seconds for it to sink in that I had just met the patron of the château.

Cyrille Portalis seemed the antipode of aristocracy—a compact man with rubbery, weathered facial features, the faint traces of a scar on his forehead, and a pattern of baldness on his crown. He had short thick fingers, and though he was barely forty at the time, he looked a good fifteen years older. If Portalis were cast in a film about revolutionary France, he would play a pitchfork-wielding peasant farmer storming the château, not anyone from his own family.

In fact, Portalis was born Cyrille de la Grandeville from another noble clan. At three he was adopted by his great-aunt, the Baroness Portalis, who was unwed and wanted to put the boy in her line of succession. The baroness and her daughter, Countess Arlette Portalis, moved from Paris to the family farm in Saint-Cyr at the outbreak of World War II. The following year, Hitler's army—fearful of an Allied landing near Toulon—stationed about four hundred troops with tanks and heavy weaponry on the family farm, ripping up vines, requisitioning crops, and building blockhouses. After the war the countess joined other family domains here in replanting mourvèdre. "She believed," Portalis said, "that wines were living and that you must respect them and give them time . . . and that wine is made in the vines."

Young Cyrille Portalis studied wine at a lycée in Beaune. After several internships in Burgundy, Bordeaux, and the Loire Valley, as well as a trip to California, he began running Pradeaux in 1983 at the age of nineteen. Since that time, working with a couple of full-time workers and seasonal hands, he has produced wines exported to two dozen countries.

We walked through a weathered wood door in Pradeaux's courtyard and into his winery—a cramped dark place with small piles of machine parts, assorted hosing, and cobwebs among huge wood aging barrels or *foudres* (dozens of times larger than fifty-nine-gallon Bordeaux barriques).

At first, I thought, Portalis had inherited none of the famed Portalis's skills as a brilliant communicator and gifted lawyer. He seemed awkward and shy around a visitor. But the more he spoke about wine, the more passionate he became in his advocacy and the more his facial features stretched into animated expressions to underline his points.

In Bandol the vines used to make red wines must be a minimum of eight years old. Portalis uses only vines that are a minimum of fifteen years old (and as old as sixty) for reds. Younger vines are used for rosé, which make up only about 20 percent of his production. He uses no herbicides or pesticides, adding only the essentials of organic viticulture: manure with treatments of sulfur and copper-based *bouille bordelaise* to guard against mildew diseases and rot. That morning Portalis and his workers were out hand-trimming the vines, eliminating the new shoots of the most productive areas of vineyards that would make the vines bushy and overproductive and ultimately dilute the wine.

Portalis is one of the few winemakers in Bandol who do not de-stem the grapes used in making their wines—sticking with the rustic practice of throwing whole grape bunches into his vats for fermentation. "I am on old dinosaur," he says. Modern conventional wisdom professes that grape stems make wines taste grassy and require more aging before drinking. Portalis explained that because of the mourvèdre grape's late maturation cycle, the stems are brown ("practically wood") at harvest and therefore don't give the wine that "green" flavor. They impart important tannins, Portalis said, unconcerned those tannins might mean his clients would have to wait a few years before drinking his red wine.

"Tomorrow, if I started to de-stem, Châteaux Pradeaux would not be the same thing," Portalis said, fixing me in his stare. "Nowadays everybody wants everything quickly. But wine is like a life: it has its youth, its apogee, and its slow decline."

After the grapes are lightly crushed, they are placed in a series of four cement fermentation tanks built into the foundation that holds up the floors and walls of the farmhouse above. A natural yeast derived from local mourvèdre is used for the first vat only. ("After that the yeast is in the air," Portalis says.) The walls of these tanks—about thirty-one inches thick—provide better insulation than any steel tanks, Portalis repeated several times. With a system of hoses and what looks like a small swimming pool pump, Portalis circulates the wine from the bottom to the top of his tanks and over the hard cap twice a day during this primary fermentation.

At the end of this period, wine is separated into *vin de goutte* (the most potent wine that runs off without pressing) and *vin de presse* (the liquid that comes from running through a press). These wines are separated for secondary fermentation and aged until the final blend is made three years later.

When it comes to the basic processes involved in winemaking, there was little to differentiate Pradeaux from many other handcrafted wines. Yet Portalis was intent on describing the chemical transformation of wine in detail, speaking faster and more passionately as he went on. It was funny, I thought: huge multinational winemakers with state-of-the art operations that more resemble refineries love to talk about the folklore of their vineyards. And here was Portalis, folklore personified with almost no modern equipment, giving a science lecture.

He explained how the vin de presse had to be warmed slightly, using a small electrode heater that is dropped into the tank, to ferment the residual sugars. And then he drew an imaginary graph on a wall to explain the thermoregulation process during fermentation.

"This is density," he said, drawing a vertical line in the air. "This is temperature," he said, making an imaginary horizontal line. He studied my face to make sure I was getting this: "This is important," he interjected. He then explained that the density decreased (downward diagonal) as temperature goes up (upward diagonal). I copied his "graph" down on my notepad. He surveyed it like a critical professor, then took the pen from my hand and added a small plateau to my "temperature" line (indicating a peak) followed by a downward diagonal.

I really had no idea what he was talking about. But only after he was sure that my graph was correct could we move around the corner to the *chais* where Portalis aged his red wines in oak foudres—actually, many of them were eighty-year-old German beer casks purchased by the estate in the 1960s.

"Never new wood," he said. "Never."

I was almost afraid to ask why, but I did.

"Mourvèdre doesn't need it," Portalis said, explaining that wine is an equilibrium of four elements: alcohol, acidity, tannins, and *matière* such as flesh and fat. "Why take a wine that is already well balanced and unbalance it?"

Still, Portalis believes that aging wine in those four-inch-thick wood barrels is necessary because wood breathes—allowing the wine to slowly oxidize and evolve. The Bandol minimum requirement for barrel aging is eighteen months. Portalis doubles that to three years. "Eighteen months isn't enough," he said. "The wines are not evolved. The tannins are too strong . . . It's not the same thing."

Only after three to four years does Portalis make the final blend of wine that goes into the Pradeaux bottle. Since 1987, at the insistence of his American importer Neal Rosenthal, Portalis stopped filtering his wines. "I am not a fan of filtering anyway," Portalis said, "It destroys the charm of a wine."

Hours had now passed in what seemed like minutes. Portalis took me around the corner where bottles covered with dust sat stacked in primitively made cubbies. These, he said, were bottles of Châteaux Pradeaux that dated back to the war. Everything from before, he lamented, the Germans took: "Les salauds ils ont tout bu!" (The bastards drank everything!) Portalis then returned to his previous train of thought, describing how wine evolves in the bottle.

"When you open a bottle and pull the cork and—poof!" He simulated this movement. "You notice that there is just a little, tiny bit of smoke that appears around the rim of the bottle. And you realize that there is a ton of reactions going on inside—a ton of reactions that the oenologists with all the research that has been done in oenology still can't describe." He paused and added, "It's a mystery."

I've never noticed any smoke coming out of any bottle. Was Portalis such a maniacally keen observer? Or truly nuts? It was evening and all that was left to do was to taste wine. I was eager to open a bottle and watch the smoke appear.

But Portalis said that tasting wine so late in the day was useless. One must taste wine before lunch—certainly about 10:30 to 11 o'clock. "Are you in a hurry?" he asked. "Can you come back one morning?"

Several attempts for a second tasting visit did not pan out. Portalis got busy. Then I got busy. Spring turned to summer to the vendanges of fall and then the Christmas holidays. I next actually spoke to Portalis on a Monday in early January the following year, 2006. I had left a message the previous week proposing that I come visit him the following day.

But, he said, the next day would not be good, he had a doctor's appointment. He had a cold. Besides, he said, it was not the best time of year to taste wine. "They are closed at this time of year. They are cold. Frozen. It can be done, but it is not optimum. Are you in a hurry?"

Not wanting to wait another eight months, I pinned Portalis down to the last day of the month.

It turned out to be a perfect warm, sunny winter morning following five days of rain in southern France. Portalis wore a brown wool sweater almost entirely covered with pilled-up balls of fuzz. We walked the vines around the winery, Portalis explaining that in an earlier age the sea had covered his land, and left behind sand and smoothed stones.

During the war, he explained, "the Germans destroyed everything. Twenty years later we were still finding artillery shells like this in the soil." He held his hands apart a good foot.

We walked through the rows of mourvèdre planted by him and his aunt in the red-orange clay and stone soils. We discussed the tending of the vines and at more than one point Portalis spoke fondly of how *les anciens* (the people of another time) "were smarter than today." "They knew when to plant vines, when to cut," he said. "Nowadays, that's all lost. People cut too early. They plant too late. They do *n'importe quoi* [whatever]."

We walked back to the winery about an hour later and Portalis retrieved a bottle of his latest vintage, the 2001, which had turned out to be a high-alcohol fruit and earth "monstre." I told him that I wanted to witness the "smoke" of the cork, and, as he pulled it, both of us stared into the neck.

"Nothing," Portalis said. He then pushed his eye closer as though staring into a microscope. "*Bon.* When I say smoke, I don't mean smoke, *smoke*, but there is sometimes that certain mist, a certain . . . *trouble.*"

What was amazing was that it was 2006 and Portalis's latest vintage of red for sale was 2001—putting him a full year behind the grandest of grand cru Bordeaux that were already selling 2002s. "We are going against the modern tendency . . . We believe, as the expression goes, in giving time its time."

Portalis went through another door and returned with an old carafe full of water spots. He poured the wine into the carafe, then left it to rest on the edge of an old stone sink while we went into the winery. Portalis used a ladder to climb onto one of those large casks or foudres. Then with a piece of rubber hosing, he sucked up enough wine to begin the flow and siphoned the liquid into a pair of glasses.

This first sample was from a parcel of 2004 mourvèdre. It smelled of fruit, but the aftertaste was bitter. "That will change," Portalis said. "It's not *animal* yet, but that will come. It is characteristic of mourvèdre when it ages."

Animal refers to a range of aromas and tastes that whiff of barnyard or the flavor of smoking meat or leather, which in small doses can be exquisite.

We moved down the row of barrels to 2003 mourvèdre and Portalis repeated the ritual. This, of course, was the famous year of record scorching heat and fires, and this wine burst out as soon as it entered the mouth, with big round fruit wrapped in a taste of tanned hide: *animal*.

Animal is something that was once thought by some to be a defect in wine. In recent times, producers in the New World and Old have tried to conjure it. I've read and heard many explanations for what delivers animal flavors—tannins in the grape skins and seeds, wild yeasts that thrive in old wood barrels, the age of the vines, and the soil geology. Exactly what molecule did Portalis theorize put the animal in Bandol wines?

Portalis was set to climb another barrel. He twisted his features in a knot, held up his hands, and shrugged. Here was a man who had probably thought more about chemistry than some chemists. And for all those decades of observations, he was left once again with the mystery, the real-or-imagined "smoke" around the opening of the bottle, which at this moment didn't seem like madness.

FIVE

A Brother's Blood

WHEN WE ARRIVED BACK AT OUR HOTEL in Calvi on Good Friday evening, there was an "urgent" message waiting. This was shocking news on several counts. First, after spending more than a week on Corsica—from its pristine coasts to its rugged mountain interior to Calvi and one of the most magnificent bays in the Mediterranean—we were on island time. Second, in Corsica hardly anyone is ever urgent about anything. And third, no one knew where we were staying. Because it was the off-season, we hadn't even made reservations.

The woman at the desk handed me the note asking that I call Monsieur Acquaviva as soon as possible. Pierre Acquaviva was an affable man with an advanced degree in medieval literature, who for the last ten years had run his family's Domaine d'Alzipratu wine property. That morning, my wife and son and I had visited the domain, which covers sixty acres of granite hills with views of the imposing Monte Grosso in one direction, and in the other, Balagne hills and the sea.

Our conversation had been mostly about wine: Corsican grapes such as the tannic niellucciu (a close relative of sangiovese, the dominant grape of Tuscany and its Chianti) and the lighter sciaccarellu that flavor northern Corsica's reds, the bad weather (too wet at the end of 2002; too dry in the spring of 2003), and the pride Pierre takes in his chemical-free Corsican terroir.

The Patrimonio appellation at the base of the Cap Corse—the island's northern peninsula—was known for producing Corsica's best-known and sturdiest reds. But along the northwestern coast of

6. Good Friday procession in Calvi, Corsica

Calvi, ten producers, including Acquaviva, were working to make a mark in their own appellation. "There's a return to tradition here," Pierre had explained. He was eloquent, mild-mannered, small with fine features. "We don't want to make international wines that are the same as the wines in Chile or South Africa. We make Corsican wines."

The sunbaked slopes of the Balagne generally provide lots of wind and sometimes no water. Making wine here was difficult but often produced spectacular results—fruit-dominated wines in which you can sometimes smell Corsica's wild brush of herbs, olives, flowers, and scrub known here as the *maquis*. These are easy-drinking wines that seem made to wash down with Corsican charcuterie, which is some of the most varied and flavorful in the world—made from mostly free-range pigs that live on an island diet of chestnuts, acorns, and fruits. The language used to describe these meats conjures another world from continental France or Italy—a world that is more rooted in common Latin and devoid of the cultural flourishes of the academies: *coppa* (made from pork loin), *lonzu* (tenderloin), *figatellu* (pork liver), *prizuttu* (the haunch). Hunting is a way of life in Corsica. Driving through the countryside and breaking for goats, cattle, and wild boar, we noticed the bilingual road signs announcing the names of places in both French and Corsican. The French signs, it seemed in some areas, were typically used for target practice and pummeled with shot. I don't hunt, but it's hard not to think of Corsican wines as an accompaniment to the hunt—or at least to be served outdoors, with meats or fish cooked over wood coals.

We'd sat outside the family farmhouse in the morning sun at a table fashioned out of a weathered piece of plywood. Behind us was a small vegetable garden with chickens running around in it. In front of us were rows of vines that tumbled down the hills toward the sea. Up the hill was an old convent used by Italy's Agnelli family, of Fiat, as a vacation home. In fact, Pierre had recounted, the now deceased Giovanni Agnelli had once come by with his friend Henry Kissinger and sipped rosé at this same makeshift table.

We'd gone down to the hangar where Pierre makes his wines: a simple, modern, but low-tech operation with stainless steel vats and no wood—oak barrels being a foreign concept from what Corsicans call "the continent." That morning we tasted some delightful rosés—the pale, uncomplicated sorts that tend to vanish on long, warm afternoons with friends. My son joined in (his first wine tasting at eight years old), filling his mouth with wine and then running outside into the vines to spit.

The winter before, I had tasted some of Domaine d'Alziptratu's reds back in Nice along with the local sommeliers association. The group notes described the 2000 vintage as a wine with powerful attack, supple, an engaging *vin de plaisir* (literally, "a pleasure wine"). This was a wine, one of the sommeliers had offered with the usual flourish, to be served with pigeon or partridge.

Regrettably, that morning when I had asked Pierre about it, he told us he was out of stock. He did have some 2002, but that, he said, was *pas terrible*—one of those French expressions that means the opposite of what it seems, meaning in this case "not great."

Then Pierre scampered up a ladder into some rafters, moved

some boxes around, and produced a bottle of 2000 red Cuvée Fiumesecco. Though he didn't have any left to sell, he could surely open just one. And that he did. It was as I remembered: lots of fruit, melting tannins, and a spicy kick. After the ceremonial nods of appreciation, Pierre offered the bottle to us to take to lunch.

Before we said our goodbyes, my wife had commented on how beautiful we had found Corsica and its coast. In our time on the island, we'd felt as though we'd entered a Mediterranean land far different from "the continent." It was miraculously free of high-rises, theme parks, and golden arches—resembling the photos of coastal Provence taken a century ago. "Yes, the coast is beautiful," Pierre had said, "but the beauty has come at a price. . . . It is beautiful because of *plastique*."

A bit of translation is needed here. In Corsica *plastique* doesn't refer to plastic superficiality or credit cards; it refers to the medium of choice among Corsican nationalists and separatists. (See "plastic explosives.") These separatists were fond of flattening French government offices and plastic-blasting most any outsider development or would-be Club Med–style vacation villages. From what I knew about the Corsican separatist movement, its philosophy seemed to be a particular blend of Green Party environmentalism and Basque-style nationalism with a page from Don Corleone's business plan. (See "protection rackets.")

It's a movement pretty well steeped in wine. After the end of the Algerian war in the 1960s, France relocated former colonists, or *pieds noirs*, from Algeria to Corsica, and helped cultivate Corsica's eastern plain for winemaking and fruit production with the help of irrigation and pesticides. In 1975 a group of about thirty Corsican nationalists—armed with hunting rifles and under the lead of a local doctor, Edmund Simeoni—occupied a pied noir's wine cellar in Aléria. The nationalists were protesting the government subsidies that benefited these outsiders who, it was argued, were unfairly using *chaptilization* (the adding of sugar before fermentation to boost alcohol content—generally reserved for gloomy northern climes like Beaujolais). Putting tactics aside, purely from a wine standpoint, the nationalists were absolutely correct—adding sugar to wine grapes in a sunny climate like Corsica's is a crime. Nevertheless, the French government, under the direction of then prime minister Jacques Chirac, called in 2,000 troops. A shootout ensued that left two gendarmes dead. Simeoni was sentenced to eighteen months in prison, and soon after being freed, he began a long career as an island politician.

That thirty-year-old dispute over tricked-up wine still hasn't been settled today, despite the French government's efforts to give Corsica semi-autonomy. This is not surprising, given that Corsicans have a reputation for being as bullheaded and combative as the island's most famous son, Napoleon Bonaparte.

After the winery shootout, the separatist FLNC (Front de Liberation National de la Corse) was formed and began its campaign of bombing government targets, exploding the work sites of chain hotels and vacation villages, or carrying out the occasional assassination or incineration of a tourist coach. But for a bunch that has been branded as terrorists, they have been meticulous about not physically harming civilians.

In fact, most Corsicans don't really want independence. Their lives and tourism-based economy are too dependent on the rest of France. Most are content to lionize the heroes of Corsica's fourteen years of independence in the eighteenth century (following five hundred years under Genoa, Italy), to fly the black and white Corsican flag (depicting a Moor's head and symbolizing the island's defeat of ancient invaders), or to keep alive the Corsican language, which is closer to Italian than French.

Pierre's comment equating beauty with bombs was delivered matter-of-factly. Of the tens of thousands of quotes I've taken down in more than twenty years of writing journalism, this is the one I recall most often.

That noontime we'd gone off to a place he'd recommended. At Chez Michel in the village of Calenzana, a barrel-chested proprietor greeted locals—both men and women—with a pair of cheek-brushing kisses. When we explained where we had just come from, there was no argument about importing our own bottle of wine. The menu included wild boar and spaghetti and whole *loup* (sea bass), caught that morning and cooked in a wood oven—all at prices less than half of what they were charging at the tourist joints on the port in Calvi.

In short, it had been a perfect, cloudless day in paradise. I had no idea why Pierre would be calling.

I phoned the number scrawled on the piece of paper and learned that it was not Pierre calling, but his father, Maurice, who said we needed to talk—just name the time and place. I was now even more bewildered. What would Maurice want from me and how did he find me? I told him to come by our hotel on the port at six.

At seventy-two, Maurice Acquaviva is the older version of his son—compact and lean with a crop of light curly hair and lively green eyes. Unlike his son, his French carries a heavy Corsican accent, and there is one other striking difference. When I put out my right hand to shake his, he intercepted it with his left hand, and shook hands awkwardly. I looked at his right hand. Sticking out from his shirtsleeve was a green plastic prosthetic hand and forearm.

He arrived early and suggested we walk across the small stone street to a place we could talk undisturbed. We went through a door off the street and mounted a staircase into a classically bourgeois-looking apartment with a vaulted dining room and high windows obscured by white lace curtains. The place belonged to a cousin, he said. We sat in red silk chairs, and Maurice explained that I should know some history that I might share with my fellow Americans. He knew that I was writing for an influential American newspaper. I explained in French that I wrote travel stories, and that I was more concerned with wine and food than with Corsican politics.

Ignoring my protests, he started with the conquest of independent Corsica by France more than two hundred years ago and for the next hour railed against the abuses of the French, from its eighteenth-century wars to its twentieth-century taxes on Corsican wines to the current service by the state-run ferry that connects the island to the mainland.

That ferry system, which took half a day to cross from Corsica to Marseille, made exportation of Corsican wines to the mainland expensive and also made it ridiculously expensive to bring in bottling materials from France. "For us to buy a bottle, the ticket, cork, and capsule costs six francs," he said. Like most people of a certain age living in France, he was destined to speak for the rest of his life in the old currency that was replaced by the euro in 2002. "But here at the supermarket they sell Bordeaux wine at the supermarket for six francs. It's the same bottle and ticket and everything but with wine inside! How can that be?"

"They have a monopoly. They have done things to keep us poor and on our knees," he spat. "The French, the *colons* (colonists) they . . ." His voice trailed off. His eyes were suddenly red. And he took his thumbnail and pushed up under his chin with it until the end of his thumb turned white.

Maurice Acquaviva then fumbled to steady a pack of cigarettes on his leg with his prosthetic plastic hand. He pulled a cigarette out with his good hand, placed it between the prosthetic fingers, and held a lighter to it. Once the cigarette was lit he removed it from the prosthesis with his left hand and began to smoke.

"Chirac has nothing to say to the United States," he blurted, now about to draw a comparison between the French president Jacques Chirac and the reviled-in-Europe American head of state George W. Bush. "Chirac has done in Corsica things ten times worse than Bush has done in Iraq."

Maurice, it turned out, was a Corsican separatist. Or, as he put it, a *resistant*. He was one of the public ones, he said. Behind the scenes were the *clandestins* of the FLNC who carried out the missions against the French state and the foreign (i.e., non-Corsican) profiteers. "I do not know them, and if I did I could not say I did, but we think the same way."

Pierre had told me about the death of his older brother, Jean Battiste, who had preceded Pierre at the winery. But I knew nothing of the circumstances. "Jean Battiste was one of the *clandestins*," Maurice said. "He was a bomber."

Maurice breathed. I looked at the lace curtains and noticed the change in evening Mediterranean light with its yellow-orange glow.

So, when he was not overseeing the vines or the family's wine-making operation, Maurice's eldest son would *plastiqué* the houses of the French government colons or of "speculators" who would profit from "cementing" Corsica's coast and then make off with the loot—always being careful to make sure the houses were empty.

One morning in 1987, when Jean Battiste was twenty-seven, he went out on a mission "to take out a house." "But someone was waiting for him. He was killed by a bullet," Maurice explained. "We don't know who did it. It was the police or the colon who lived there. We asked the court to investigate how he was killed. But they never did anything."

As Maurice went on, I was struck by his description of his son's errand of blowing up a house—delivered in the same casual tone that one might say, "He went out for a loaf of bread one morning . . . "

By the time Maurice finished his story, I felt drained. Hours had passed. I summoned the courage to ask Maurice the awkward question. How had he lost his hand? Had that too been a bombing mission?

He looked at his prosthetic, and then moved as if it were capable of making a waving motion that would minimize his physical circumstances. It was a boyhood wound, he explained, the result of his playing with an Italian army grenade after the occupation of World War II.

It was our last night on Corsica. The next morning we would be taking a ferry back to Nice. Over dinner that evening at a romantic inn on the outskirts of town, my cell phone sounded. I fumbled with it as I stood and hurried out to the lobby where I answered the call.

It was Acquaviva the elder. He wanted to make sure I observed the Good Friday processions in Calvi that evening. Yes, I told him, we were planning to be there. We said goodbye for the second time in a matter of hours.

In fact, the traditional Good Friday processions had been on my mind all day. In the newspaper that morning the top story announced that a teenager had been killed and another injured while handling plastic explosives near Bastia. The other big story was the continuation of the Holy Week celebrations. Corsica's fervor for Catholic rituals is legendary—one more way it differentiates itself from the cynical and fiercely secular mainland.

Throughout Corsica, dozens of processions that evening would remember Christ's march up Calvary using anonymous penitents and bearing large wooden crosses. Details of the marches varied: in some cases the penitents walked in foot chains; they were always barefoot and hooded.

After dinner we found the procession as it was leaving the port in Calvi and heading through town. Hundreds of people, following a group of robed priests, church deacons, and altar boys, chanted "Miserere Domine" through the stone streets. At the front of the group, two penitents—each shrouded in a white cotton hood and robe—shouldered a single wooden cross; they seemed to be struggling under the weight of the wood beams and the pressure of the cobblestones underfoot. Following the pair was a group of men carrying a plaster-cast Christ—in what seemed his last gasp of life—on a bed of flowers. The next group carried a plaster statue of the Virgin in black mourning clothes.

In Calvi tradition, the procession entered public squares and then coiled in on itself in a snail pattern. The circle grew as tight as possible, and then it slowly uncoiled without a break in the chanting.

For hours the group crossed the city, which sits on two levels connected by steep stone streets: the port facing the Bay of Calvi and Corsica's interior, and the walled citadel built six centuries ago on a promontory, between the bay and the sea, looking out in all directions toward the city's enemies.

As we watched the methodical coiling and uncoiling at the foot of Calvi's heavily fortified walls, I noticed lit candles set out on what seemed to be every doorway and window. I asked a woman from Calvi, Who were these hooded men? They were locals, she said, selected by the parish priest to purge a sin. It's a job that is sought after, she informed me. In Corsica on Good Friday, there is no shortage of volunteers.

A Brother's Blood 87

SIX

Drinking with Uncle Jacques

I'D FIRST MET JACQUES on a family trip to France. At the time, our home was on a shaded street in Fort Worth. Our son, at four years old, spoke French with his mother but considered himself Texan, and we hadn't seriously considered moving to another continent.

Jacques, the older brother of my wife's deceased father, was a retired construction engineer. He was born near Toulouse, and as a young man he worked with the French army's civil corps in central Africa. He later returned to Paris with his wife, Jeanne, and an adopted son to build a career. Jacques had recently retired and was living near Versailles.

This trip marked the first time my wife, Gilda (pronounced "Jilda" after Rigoletto's daughter), had seen her uncle since she was a small girl. Gilda was born in Nice when both her parents were still in their teens. Her father, the adventurous son of a decorated French army colonel, did not hang around. Her parents divorced, and her father took to sea and rarely visited. Years later, after her mother had remarried and settled in California, my wife learned that the boat her father was captaining for an Italian shipping company had disappeared off the coast of Sicily. "We're not exactly close" is how she usually described family relations.

Our first morning in Paris, Jacques met us at our hotel, which, thanks to one of those family-fun-in-Paris airline package deals, was located in out-of-the-way Pigalle, where it seemed sex shops, streetwalkers, and transvestites outnumbered tourists who might fancy Paris's more subtle charms.

At the time, Jacques was in his mid-sixties with a bulge around

7. Uncle Jacques and the backdrop of "le Canigou" from Château Mossé

his midsection a bit too large to be considered a mere tire. Two fenders of thin white hair bulged from the sides of his bald crown. He wore a navy sweater-vest and carried a leather pouch—no doubt for those oversized French documents such as his driver's license and checkbook. He was the picture of an old-school professional in what the French politely call the *troisième âge* (third age).

After a series of embraces and French let-me-look-at-yous, we climbed in Jacques's well-polished Citroën sedan. He told us that he had been surprised by the location of our accommodations. It was not usually, he said—giving me a once-over—a place where Americans stay.

Within minutes we were on the autoroute to Versailles, where we walked the famous gardens. Jacques pointed out the old engineering academy where he had studied as a young man. When we arrived at the small, tidy suburban home nearby, I was struck by the smell of something meaty and delicious wafting from the kitchen.

Jeanne and Jacques had a similar look and shape—a phenomenon

I attributed to their forty years of marriage. They both stood about five feet four with rounded bodies balanced atop small feet. Their soft, pale faces were bespectacled with the same style of large, and dated, gold-rimmed glasses.

On their dining table draped in Old World lace, Jeanne served us one of those simple but extraordinary Sunday lunches the French expect as a way of life. I remember the main dish as being a stewed chicken smothered in mushrooms, but neither the chicken nor the mushrooms smelled or tasted like their standard American counterparts. The meat had just enough gaminess to resemble something that had actually come from a living creature; the mushrooms were profoundly earthy. The bird was surely farm raised and was probably purchased with its head and a few stray feathers intact—not one of those colorless critters that look and taste as if they were born in the fluorescent glare of the supermarket meat section. The mushrooms were *cèpes* that Jacques had picked himself and frozen that winter. The wine was from some Bordeaux appellation, perhaps Saint-Émilion.

We spoke about family and plans for our vacation traversing the country. At some point the subject of French cuisine came up. To me, at the time, it was all French food, and as long as you stayed away from the obvious tourist mills and fast food joints, it was all good.

"Ah, but in Paris, you cannot eat well!" Jacques stated authoritatively.

I must have looked as dumbfounded as I would have if he'd announced that for an *entremet* between courses we would be nibbling on a pâté made from the family cat. Was not Paris, after all, the capital of world gastronomy?

"It's true," Jacques continued, shaking his head. "In Paris, all you can find is *la boof . . . la boof* for the tourists."

"*Boeuf?*" I said, wondering, what was the beef?

Everyone else laughed at this, my son included. My wife then explained that Jacques wasn't referring to *le boeuf* but *la bouffe*—slang for "chow" or "slop."

Jacques went on, explaining with an engineer's know-it-all that in the Paris area all the lime had long ago been stripped from the soil to make cement. You had to go outside the region to find any good soil, or terroir. Jacques then went on to praise the cuisine of southwest France, which far surpassed that of Paris.

"Besides," he added, "I am from the Southwest."

I was beginning to understand. Jacques would no more stomach a cassoulet in Paris than a Tennessean could accept New Jersey pulled pork. Multiply that by hundreds of regions, subregions, appellations, villages with their own cuisine, wine, cheese, and, in some cases, languages and you begin to get the picture of the scope of French regionalism.

Next came the large platter of cheese, mingling an array of pungent odors. Jacques refilled my wine glass. I gingerly sliced into a wheel of something that had a light bluish white crust and smelled as if it had come right out of a barn.

"Take some cheese!" Jacques insisted, mocking the dainty nouvelle cuisine morsel balanced on the edge of the knife.

"I did," I said.

"No, that's not a piece of cheese—that's a supermarket sample."

I cut a bigger wedge.

"That's more like it," Jacques said. "Voila!"

When it came Jacques's turn, he wielded the knife and made one fluid scooping motion, coming up with an oozing yellow triangular wedge. He pushed it directly into a crusty piece of baguette and bit into it.

Jacques, like nearly every French man and woman I've met from his generation, clearly enjoyed food and drink and—above all—authenticity. This was confirmed at the end of lunch when he pulled out a bottle of colorless liquid and set it on the table. The simple liter-sized bottle bore a tiny, plain white sticker. And written on it—in shaky, smudged ballpoint-blue scrawl—was the word "Calvados," the apple liquor of Normandy. One belt of this 100-proof hooch—the stuff tasted like roasted apples—was enough to make me understand why the bootlegger who made it could barely write.

The following day, before we left Paris, Jacques and Jeanne took us on a whirlwind tour of Paris's tourist clichés—the Eiffel Tower, the Seine by *bateau mouche*, Notre Dame. As night approached, I discussed dinner reservations. Jacques waved this idea off. In Paris, he insisted, one shouldn't bother trying to eat well. But, he said, he did know a place we could get decent hamburgers.

A few years later, just before we moved to France, Jacques called and told my wife that Jeanne had died. The breast cancer she'd been treated for years earlier had apparently taken root in her brain; she did not survive the radiation therapy.

For the next two years, contact by letter and telephone was sporadic. We were dealing with the inevitable complications of a transatlantic move. And for two years, Jacques barely left the house and made no effort to see anyone. In one conversation he informed Gilda that his adopted son (from Jeanne's short-lived first marriage) had cut off communications—meaning that he had lost not only a wife but also his immediate family, including three grandchildren. He would be selling his house, he said, to move close to his only surviving brother, Michel, near Perpignan in the Catalan country that straddled France and Spain.

Time passed, and in the spring of 2004 Jacques visited us in France. He looked older than his seventy years. He also seemed sadder than I'd remembered. But in spite of what he'd been through, he hadn't lost his opinionated feistiness.

I was eager to impress Jacques with my growing savoir faire in matters of food and wine. I now knew, after all, what a serving of cheese was. And my wine cellar was now filling up with bottles from all corners of France. On the night of his arrival I opened a dusty twenty-year-old vintage bottle from Saint-Émilion—part of the gesture that the mill's previous owner had made to cement the sale. I don't remember the wine as much as I remember Jacques's reaction to my serving methods.

I brought the bottle up to the kitchen. And with the sharp end of the cork, I ripped off the top of the capsule, then uncorked the bottle and upended it into a decanter. Jacques, who was standing next to me, let out a gasp—holding his hands to his head. I stopped pouring and looked down, wondering what was wrong. Was I absentmindedly pouring the wine over my shoes?

"What?" I asked Jacques.

"Slowly, gently," he said, grabbing my pouring hand and wresting the bottle from me. Jacques then lovingly cradled the bottle upright. He took a knife and redid my handiwork—evening out the edges of the torn capsule. He patiently tipped up the back end of the bottle, until the wine flowed down the inside edges of the glass without a single *glug*.

"When you wake up after a long nap, do you prefer to be waken up gently or thrown out of bed?" Jacques said. "It is the same with wine."

My crime is that I had been treating a good wine with little respect—in other words, acting like an American.

"Wines should be handled gently, or what is the point . . . ?" he went on for the next few minutes. It soon became clear that in the years since I'd last seen him, Jacques had picked up the habit of repeating himself for emphasis—at least three times.

Six months later, two weeks before Christmas, I called Jacques to tell him I would be coming to visit him for a couple of days. I proposed that the two of us take a road trip through the Roussillon vineyards. Like so many of his countrymen, Jacques loved wine, had strong opinions, and didn't give a flip what others thought—a good companion for a wine trip, I thought.

I arrived days later at Jacques's house in a plain suburban village outside Perpignan. It was a white, modern Mediterranean stucco house that shared a wall with his neighbors. Up front were a single small olive tree and the last dying remnants of a grass lawn that someone had attempted to grow in dirt that had the look of cement. Along the side of the house was a row of citrus trees—in back was a small grove of assorted dying or dead fruit trees and a line of young cypresses that Jacques had planted to hide the view of a supermarket service station and an industrial bread factory.

Inside, Jacques took me on a tour of the small two-story house, which was fastidiously kept. "Not as big as your house, of course,"

Jacques said. Reminders of Jeanne were everywhere: oil paintings she had made in Africa hanging on the walls, photos of her in every room, a bottle of her perfume sitting on a shelf in the bathroom, three pairs of her small house slippers neatly arranged in the bottom of a closet.

Jacques and I mounted the stairs, and he showed me the guest room. "Smaller than your house . . . ," he repeated. We returned downstairs to the living/dining room where Jacques was unfolding a map of Roussillon on the dining table.

"First of all, let me say that I am flattered that you as an American are interested in French *terroir*," Jacques said with an ambassador's flair he'd probably learned on one of his foreign assignments. "Because, you know, the French say that Americans don't normally eat very well."

"They say, 'Yes, the Americans sometimes eat foie gras and Roquefort, but they want everything sterilized.' And sterilized foie gras, excuse me," he chortled, "is not the same thing at all."

"And the cheese," Jacques said. "Well, American cheese is not quite cheese." Nowadays, Jacques continued, there was, of course, an overproduction of good wines in the world.

"Years ago in Roussillon all they made here was *piquette*; they called it that because it *piqued* (stung). They only cared about quantity. In recent years they have been they concentrating on quality and replacing vines, and doing what they must do to raise the standard."

Jacques pulled three tumblers out of the china cabinet and placed them carefully at chosen points on the map. He then went out to his closed-in (unheated) back porch and returned with three slightly chilled bottles, which he used to fill the three glasses.

I sat down in front of the map, and then Jacques began to fold up a plain piece of white paper. He then held his white origami page over the map, explaining it represented the topography of Roussillon, with a steep incline on the northern edge representing the Corbières, on the border with Languedoc. In the southwest was the high snow-capped mountain known as Canigou, and in the southeast, the coastal Mediterranean cliffs of Banyuls. In the middle of all this was the plain.

Jacques then explained that the three glasses contained *vins doux naturels* from three distinct areas. Roussillon is the largest producer of fortified wines in France made by a process in which grape alcohol is added to young wines to stop fermentation and maintain high residual sugar. These wines are aged in oak barrels sometimes for decades. Lighter versions tend to be drunk as before-meal aperitifs with pâté or dried sausage; the more aged varieties are often consumed after a meal like fine ports. They tend to be strong in both alcohol content and flavor, and in the modern world beyond French Catalan are somewhat out of fashion.

"Now the first one is from the plain," Jacques explained, pointing to the glass tumbler in the middle of the map. I looked at the corresponding bottle of a local Rivesaltes Ambré. The label on the back indicated it was made from macabeu and grenache blanc grapes and aged in oak barrels. As the name implies, it was a deep amber color.

At first sniff it smelled like honey. "This one is for the ladies, because they like it best," Jacques remarked.

Next we moved to Banyuls, grown on the famous cliff sides by the Mediterranean. We were still in the sweet category but the wine was a deep red brown and a bit drier.

Next we mounted the northern slopes of Jacques's map, and for the climb Jacques joined me by pouring himself a glass of Maury from the village of the same name. It looked like the Banyuls, but it was different from the first sniff. It was somehow tougher, with a smell that I imagined raw cocoa leaves must smell like (though I've never to my knowledge smelled a cocoa leaf).

"It tastes more of the *terre*," Jacques noted.

That evening we ate in Jacques's small white-painted kitchen at a 1960s-era Formica table. He sautéed some veal steaks in a pan and served them with some frozen potato cubes he popped in the oven. "I am sorry. I never learned to cook because Jeanne was such a good cook," he said.

We washed the meal down with some local red table wine grown somewhere beyond the bread factory. He told me over and over again how glad he was I'd come to visit. Since Jeanne had died, he said, the most unbearable part of his day was dinnertime.

The next morning we set out in Jacques's minivan for Maury and the southern flanks of the Corbières, a small subregion known as Fenouillèdes. First, we stopped in the plain in the nearby town of Rivesaltes at a well-reputed winery favored by both Parker (who classified the winemaker as "excellent") and the French *Guide Hachette*.

The woman who greeted us in the well-appointed tasting room at Domaine Cazes had not been expecting guests. She complained that it was out of season, and that they did not have all their stock to taste. "This time of year," she said, "isn't the best." Nevertheless, she went over to the refrigerator-sized wine cabinet and pulled out some already opened bottles.

We started with some reds. She poured a glass of traditional red: it was thin and unremarkable. Then she poured glasses of two prestige cuvées from 2001 (considered a good vintage in the region) aged in wood barrels.

As I lifted the first to my nose I smelled what I thought were the stirrings of something interesting. I sipped, slurped, swirled. I was astonished. I could taste almost nothing.

I remarked that I found the wine weaker than the first. "No, that's impossible," the woman said. Maybe I was mistaken, I thought, and sniffed and slurped a second round with no change. We verified the labels. Maybe, I offered, it was my uncle Jacques's coffee that morning that had killed my taste buds. The third wine was also on the weak and watery side.

Jacques, who had stood on the sidelines, then stepped up to the bar for a taste. "This one [the second] is weaker than this one [the first]," he said.

The woman repeated the impossibility of our perceptions. Before we left we tasted some of the domaine's vins doux, including Muscat de Rivesaltes, which were finely made with a seductive bouquet and freshness and not as cloying as many sweet wines.

As you leave the plain and drive up the valley of the River Agly, the terrain quickly becomes rocky and rugged. The vineyards change from the seas of orderly flatland rows planted in hard mud to steep terraces and vine rows that seem to sprout from rock.

Above us along the mountain ridge, occasionally peeking through the winter cloud cover that filled the sky that day, were a series of castles and fortifications in varying states of ruin. Once Cathar outposts, Jacques explained, they were used by a succession of French kings as defensive garrisons and lookouts over the plain.

At one point we pulled up to a winery below a large, bright terra cotta–colored "château" built into the hillside. Here at the charmingly named Château de Jau (another Parker favorite), Jacques said, he and Jeanne used to buy wine together when visiting the area.

A lone employee, surrounded by large stainless steel wine tanks, puddles, and large industrial hosing in the large hangar that appeared to be a winery, greeted us and led us into a tiny office with a sink and stacked cases of wine. He poured us some samples of nothing remarkable and then went on to complain about how badly the winery—he nodded toward the area with puddles and hoses—needed updating and repair.

He noted that the owners—the Davré family, who owned other properties in Roussillon—focused more of their attention on their new winery in Chile, which was another world, a *merveille* (marvel) with state-of-the-art everything. Before we left, he asked where we were headed next. "Up," I told him, pointing up the valley.

He told us that if were looking for dry red wines "they are doing some incredible things in Caramany."

"Where?" I asked. Caramany, Jacques explained, was at the top of the river valley.

As we visited wineries that day, Jacques developed a pattern. Before we entered a place, Jacques would say, "You just handle everything; I will say nothing." But then, usually, after the first "bonjour" he would take over, explaining to whoever was helping us that I was an American journalist doing an *étude* of the regional wines, and so on. Once such formalities were out of the way, Jacques generally had no problem diving headlong into conversation and delivering his own critiques, opinions, and sometimes advice.

We arrived at Maury just after noon. After filling our stomachs with plates of grilled meat at a storefront restaurant on the main route into town, we drove to Mas Amiel, a highly regarded Maury producer owned since 1999 by Olivier Decelle, the former president of France's giant frozen-food store chain, Picard. Decelle wasn't likely to be around, having recently purchased the Saint-Émilion grand cru Château Jeane-Faure. At Mas Amiel he had received favorable press in France for renovating the winery, bringing in new money and a new wine team, and turning the whole operation biodynamic.

On a terrace just below the winery were a couple of thousand *bonbonnes*—those large round glass flasks (in this case one hundred liters) that are the traditional staple of the French countryside—used for storing everything from olive oil to *eau de vie* (fruit brandy). They appeared to be filled with murky liquids—tens of thousands of gallons of the stuff.

We knocked at the door of the office and were met by Laurent Moinet, a youngish man, in perhaps his late thirties, whose card described him as an *attaché commercial* (a salesman). Moinet led us to Mas Amiel's tasting bar. Jacques, of course, introduced me and my mission in Maury. He then recounted for Moinet—in detail that tested the younger man's patience—how we had prepared a tasting of vins doux the night before at his dining table.

Moinet, politely waiting for Jacques to finish, explained that Maury suffers harsh winters on the flanks of Corbières with legendary winds that whistled down the river valley. The vines suffered and, as a result, developed hardier root systems that in turn produced more concentrated grapes with their mark of terroir.

One of the techniques used by Mas Amiel involved those bonbonnes we saw up front: as part of a centuries-old practice, the sweet wines were left outdoors for a full year to bake in the summer sun and shiver all winter. Another technique involved leaving the Catalan macabeau grapes on the rocks to dry for weeks before collecting them.

Jacques and I walked around the tasting room while Moinet prepared a tasting. The wines were attractively packaged in skinny cylindrical bottles with modern graphics, bright-colored labels, and relatively big price tags. At one point Jacques nudged me as he looked at a half bottle of vin doux from 1980 that was selling for forty euros. "Do you see that?" he whispered, not quite as discreetly as he thought. "*C'est cher!*" (Expensive!)

We began tasting the lineup of wines that Moinet had put out along the bar. With each wine, served at a cool temperature, I detected another explosion of fruit and alcohol in the mouth.

Jacques sniffed and sipped the samples without offering a word. When I made a spontaneous "mmmmm" sound to express my delight with Mas Amiel's vintage Maury, Jacques responded with a cropped "nnnh"—the French way of saying nothing and making a point at the same time. Depending on the context, this short nasal punctuation can mean either "Amen" or "That's really bullshit, but I'm going to hold my tongue."

Jacques and Moinet somehow launched into a conversation more important at the moment than wine—a French railing session starting on the skyrocketing prices of real estate. "The English and Germans are buying up everything!" Moinet complained. Jacques told the story of a farm he had stayed in with his family on a trip to the Pyrenees years ago. The farm sold and the new owners—English—turned a stable for animals into a house! "Can you believe it? And it was probably worth millions!"

And so it turned into a duel of anecdotes. After about twenty minutes they had vented their Gallic demons, and there was silence. Moinet asked what would be our next stop.

"Up to Caramany," I said.

"Ahh. They make some reds up there that are *costaud* [strong]," he said, flexing a bicep.

Caramany—I was now really intrigued. Who'd ever heard of Caramany? And why did it have such a local reputation?

Back in the car, just as soon as the doors were closed shut, Jacques uncorked his opinions about Mas Amiel's wine. "They are too much, too fruity, too caramel, too sugary," he declared.

He repeated variations on this theme about six times that afternoon and the following day. The wines were like a woman with too much makeup, he said. And furthermore, what was all that business about leaving the wine outside in glass? "I don't like that they cook the wines like that. I don't like that at all."

From Maury we pushed up into the hills of steeper cliffs, almost otherworldly rocky landscapes, and perilous two-way roads barely wide enough for one car through vine rows that seemed to be barely hanging onto the mountainsides. The air was colder and felt thinner.

The Caramany cooperative, a typical small-town affair, was decked out for Christmas. A woman came out and poured us some samples of Caramany—aged in wood barrels and not. The wines were inexpensive by any standard, starting at less than five euros and topping off at less than ten for the cooperative's national gold medal prestige Huguet de Caraman 2001 made from carignan and syrah.

From the first sniff, the wines had an agreeable pronounced bouquet, but in the mouth they were aggressive. This was big, tannic wine as dry as the canyons. Perhaps it was all the *doux* (sweetness) I sampled that day, but my taste buds were in shock. I couldn't really tell if I was drinking wine or antifreeze.

On the way back down toward Perpignan, we passed some rock formations reminiscent of the Grand Canyon. I commented to Jacques how much the wine tasted like the terrain.

"As hard as the rocks," Jacques said.

That evening we ate dinner at the home of Jacques's brother Michel, and we brought a bottle of Caramany along. Michel and his wife, Tinou, lived a simple country life outside Perpignan, and they weren't the kind of people to stand on ceremony. On that family trip a few years earlier, I remember my wife had scolded my son for putting his feet on their sofa. "That's okay," Tinou laughed, "we raised a baby goat on that thing."

Now that their children were grown, Tinou spent much of her time looking after a sweet-faced boy of ten. The parents were divorced and rarely had time for their child, so Tinou and Michel became his surrogate parents.

Michel was a roofing contractor, forced to take retirement when he was injured by a tile roof that had collapsed under him. He was nearly ten years younger than his older brother, and as they sat on the old sofa I realized how closely their shapes resembled each other's. When not standing, Jacques and Michel resembled a pair of plump Chinese Buddhas.

We opened the Caramany with the cheese course after a meal of roasted tenderloin. Michel, who had spent most of his life in the area, explained the significance of Caramany and the high-sloped mountainsides above the Roussillon plain.

"My father-in-law was a winemaker on the plain, and the wine he made was nothing—6 or 7 percent alcohol (about half the strength of today's Caramany) and barely red," Michel said, referring to the 1960s. "Everything was quantity, quantity and not quality. But at the end of the Algerian war, the pieds noirs came and they transformed the mountainsides and cultivated the vines up there. Nobody else wanted to go up there. The locals were all down on the plain. But they planted and cultivated the mountainsides, and that was the start of the movement to quality in Roussillon."

We drank the wine and spread oozing sheep's cheese on pieces of baguette. It was the same Caramany I had tasted earlier, but, accompanied by eye-watering cheese reminiscent of sheep's hide, it was sublime.

Michel then poured us glasses from a bottle of Maury from the village cooperative and Jacques described in detail our trip to Mas Amiel.

"It was like you took a prune, put a piece of caramel on it and ate it," he said. "I tell you, it was something else, syrup maybe. But it was not wine!"

The next morning we headed out to find the village of Sainte-Colombe-de-la-Commanderie—southwest of Perpignan in the brush-covered hills known as the Aspres. When our local map failed us, we stopped in another village to ask directions from a tall man in a red sweater.

"It's me you're looking for, I think," said Jacques Mossé, owner of Château Mossé, with whom we had scheduled a 10 a.m. rendezvous. He gave us directions to his winery and told us he would join us in twenty minutes.

All along the two-minute drive to Sainte-Colombe, I was amazed the way Mossé had picked us out. Then we arrived in Sainte-Colombe and I understood. There is really nothing in Sainte-Colombe—no bakery, no tobacconist, not a single shop—and only about fifty inhabitants. There are several things about Sainte-Colombe that stayed with me and have drawn me back.

The first and most dramatic impression is the setting. On the road that leads from the town, the landscape has been obscured by residential housing developments and expensive new villas in what were once vines. But in Sainte-Colombe itself, looking to the southwest, there is nothing but the rounded hills of the Aspres, crisscrossed with vineyards and olive groves leading out to a horizon dominated by the angular snowcapped peaks of Canigou, which glowed in a warm, bright morning light.

We walked to the edge of town and then into the vine rows planted in red clay laced with white and pink quartz. Then we walked every inch of the town, where we found under the tall Mediterranean pines the second wonder of Sainte-Colombe: the walls.

The town's centuries-old walls are constructed in Catalan style—mixing the local varieties of stone and marble—with thumb-sized pieces of brick. The overall effect is at once rustic and refined, and in the morning light resembles more a painter's impression than building masonry.

When we arrived at the collection of old stone buildings that formed the winery, Jacques Mossé greeted us in the drive. A tall man in his late fifties, he wore Armani jeans and hand-nursed a small cigar. The winery was established by his family in 1844, and he was the fifth generation. His father had been mayor of the town for fifty years. Mossé said Sainte-Colombe remained so well preserved because of its principal asset—a stone quarry, which provided the village with a source of income and stones.

Mossé's father had made only sweet wines: the large barrels in his cellar held special vintages dated back to 1947. In the mid-1980s, Mossé said, he made his first reds. Now his principal exports were in Europe, notably Belgium. Mossé then led us to his tasting room, a small stone room with a fountain for spitting made from what looked like an old stone pig trough.

We started with the reds, and from the first contact with Mossé's under-five-euros 2003 red, it was clear we had found something. This wasn't a generic weakling from lowlands, or a pumped-up black wine from the mountain cliffs, but a smooth, easy-drinking violet-colored wine that seemed to reflect those gentle red slopes.

As we moved up the chain of his wines into his barrel-aged reds, I smelled and tasted one of the most welcome surprises sometimes found in Roussillon reds (especially in old carignan vines): tobacco. I am not a smoker and avoid tobacco smoke, but Mossé's wines conjured a fine, unlit cigar.

In exceptional years, he vinified a wine made exclusively from more than 100-year-old carignan vines. The year 2003—the summer of France's infamous heat wave, or *canicule*—had been that kind of year. He led us out to his cellar and a row of old barriques (he uses aged wood barrels rather than new wood), explaining it would not be in bottles until February. He stuck a pipette into one barrel, withdrawing enough wine for all three of us to sample.

It was the kind of wine that makes French sommeliers gush about animal essences, tobacco, and herbs.

"*Excusez-moi*," Jacques stated, ceremoniously pulling his nose out of the glass. "But I will not spit."

None of us did.

We returned to Mossé's tasting room, where he started pulling out his sweet vins doux. We started with Rivesaltes, that sweet amber-colored wine made mostly from grenache. It was more subtle—less sugary and explosive—than anything we had tasted on this trip. Jacques slowly let some of the nectar roll back into his mouth and down his throat. Then he pronounced softly, "This is cream."

Mossé then opened a bottle of his 1976 vintage Rivesaltes—which had twenty years of barrel aging before bottling.

The three of us drank in silence. Jacques closed his eyes for more than a few seconds. When he opened them, he had the look of a man who had been moved on some deep level. It was as if the wine had reached inside him and touched some nerve ending of emotion or unearthed a shard of memory. In an instant those narrow eyes behind his glasses dampened.

When we left, we headed out to the nearby town of Thuir, where Mossé had recommended a local family-run restaurant. At La Taverna del Galet we ate snails in spicy Catalan sauce, followed by meats grilled over coals in the dining room hearth. We were one of the only tables in the place, but that didn't arrest the festive atmosphere. After the meal the restaurant chef brought us a Catalan flask, a *porron*, of pale muscat. Perceiving that I was American, and that I had no idea what to do with this flask that looked like it came directly out of a chemistry lab, he offered a demonstration.

A porron looks like a bulbous wine decanter with a thick neck that is bent to one side. On the opposite side is a long, thin spout designed to emit the finest trickle of liquid. The trick is to never let the spout touch your lips, but to actually make the stream go in one's mouth.

The chef, who was a man about my age, took the porron, held it up to the ceiling, and poured out a long, arcing stream into his open mouth. Then he flexed his arm up and down—shortening and lengthening the stream without straying from his target. He then offered to pay for our meal if I could follow his example and drink from the flask without spilling the wine. Now, all eyes in the place were on me.

I lifted the porron, attempting something that could be called casual confidence. I held it high overhead, tilted my head back, and poured the muscat over my face and shirtfront. The chef, staff, and other guests clapped. More porrons appeared. And for the first time that I could remember, Jacques laughed—a long, uncontrolled laugh that went from his belly to his eyes, which filled with tears. He removed his glasses.

Later I thought about the other tears Jacques had produced that day in reaction to Mossé's last wine—the one that followed the wine he had pronounced to be "cream." I never asked him about it, though I had an idea what—or whom—it had touched inside of him.

After that long silence, he had finally spoken. "And this," he'd said, "is cream for her majesty."

SEVEN

Poop and People in the
New French Wine Country

DIDIER BARRAL STOMPED ON THE BRAKE of his old Citroën Deux-Chevaux just in front of his winery's shitpile. Off to the side of a washed out road of sand and stone, sat several tons of manure lightly steaming in the crisp January morning.

"Ça," Barral turned to me and said, gesturing toward the pile, "c'est important." At thirty-nine and sturdily built with thick whitish hair, Barral had a habit of emphasizing what was important in his deep Occitan accent. He spoke the word *important* not in the pointed, precise Parisian style from the front of the lips. Rather, he let the word roll up from the back of the throat, slide over his tongue, and fall flat before it choked off. "C'est très, très *am-pour-tenh.*"

Barral went on to explain that this was no ordinary mountain of manure but a soil-nourishing cocktail of poop from animals with all the diversity of Noah's Ark: horse, sheep, pigs, goats, rabbits, birds, chickens, pigeons, and more.

Barral stepped on the gas pedal, bouncing the two of us along a path in the fragrant low-lying garrigue. When we came to a stream, Barral splashed the 2CV through it, and those worn, miniature tires pulled us up a rugged incline you'd think would necessitate some sort of off-road military vehicle that could snack on Barral's "tin snail."

"Plants need diverse food," Barral said as my intestines jumped up somewhere near my throat. "If you have a dog that eats only rabbit every day, that's no good, he will become sick. If you eat only pork every day, that's no good. . . . *C'est important.*"

8. Didier Barral, staying close to his earth

Barral stopped on a plateau covered with winter-bare vineyards in the process of being cut back to their twisted arthritic trunks. We got out of the car—Barral had other things to show me that were *important*. One of them was an immense flat cow pile. He squatted on his haunches and scrutinized it with a look that I'd call admiration.

"The manure is good, but it is not *le top*," Barral observed. "This," he said, now squatting next to the meadow muffin, "is the best."

For the last five years Barral had allowed his small herd of cattle to graze his vineyards in winter, digesting grasses and recycling them into large disks of fertilizer that he explained were more natural—and preferable—to barn manure.

"Manure is an invention of man. In nature, a cow puts his turd here and goes *pee-pee* over there," said Barral, pointing to a spot about ten yards away. "But in the barnyard an animal goes in the same place. In manure, the turd is mixed with urine and that makes ammonia that drives away the insects. . . ." And insects, Barral noted, were *très, très, très important*. As were the crows. "After we introduced the cows," he said, "the crows came and they left their turds and their feathers. . . ."

"And also we have one bull in the middle of seven cows and the cows have babies. So every three months we kill one of the calves, and the taste of the meat is [here Barral kissed his fingertips and pronounced one of the French language's greatest compliments] *terrible*."

To the north were miles on miles of regional forests that crossed miles of low-lying mountains; in all other directions were more hills and vineyards of Faugères. This winegrowing region, about twenty-five miles inland from the Mediterranean coast as it makes it final arc toward Spain, is known for its loose, flat stone soils, its cool microclimate, and complex, elegant wines that have nothing in common with the Languedoc stereotypes of red, high-octane fruit jams or industrial swill.

From here in Lenthéric—a hamlet with one stop sign, one abandoned telephone booth, and a lady in a white van who delivers baguettes and eggs most mornings—Barral has become one of the leading voices in France's movement of neo-peasant winegrowers, pursuing an agricultural revolution with Jeffersonian fervor. Though the man doesn't own a computer, Barral has developed a global following for his natural, if rustic, wines. When I visited him in the winter of 2006, Barral was preparing for his second trip to New York, where he would opine to wine professionals on the other side of the Atlantic what he considered *important*.

That morning in Barral's modest winery, an old farm building next to his house, we had spoken of the state of French terroir. And being as he was both French and a revolutionary, it was only natural that he pronounce the death of the ancien régime.

"The great *terroirs* of France, from Saint-Émilion to Montrachet," he'd said, "*ils sont morts* [they are dead]." Overuse of chemicals, fertilizers, and even products used in organic agriculture like sulfur and copper, Barral went on, had killed the soils, including those in Faugères.

Poop and People in the New French Wine Country 109

"Yes," he'd qualified, "now it's coming back because some people are making efforts, but ten years ago it was like this." He pointed to the cement floor. "Dead." And the natural life of the soil is about as important as things get in Barral's pantheon of priorities.

Barral had said his now-retired father had shunned chemicals when they came into vogue in the 1960s and 1970s. Since taking over the family vineyards and launching Domaine Leon Barral (named after his grandfather) in the early 1990s, Barral had developed a philosophy and methodology based on his own observations of nature: "What I see in the forest, I try to duplicate. . . . In nature, trees don't get sick as they do in an orchard."

It had been three years since he'd used sulfur in his vines, a common organic treatment against mildew diseases and parasites. Up until three years ago, Barral said, he had used an organic treatment to curb grape worms that attack vine flowers. He said that since then, by encouraging predators—bats, moths, spiders, birds, and ants—and by plowing his soil less, the worms had disappeared on their own.

"You have to think of *tout le monde*," Barral said. And when Barral said *tout* (everyone), he meant it. Spending time with him outdoors was like being trapped in one of those microscopic-view nature films with Barral acting as the narrator. I had up to this day looked at thousands of vine rows, admired their orderly beauty, the soil quality, exposition, and surroundings, but I'd never thought of bugs at this profound level.

At one point along a drainage ditch near a road that cut through his vines, Barral pointed out an area where the dusty earth was ever so lightly disturbed. "A trail," he noted, "for the little rats . . . That's *important*—they work the soil too."

Over the course of the hours spent visiting the vines around Lenthéric, Barral often stopped to point out the differences between his vines and those of neighbors with whom he shared hillsides.

The first thing that you notice about Barral's vines is that they are cut in the traditional goblet style, low to the ground and allowing the fruit-bearing shoots to spread in every direction. Most other vines are trained on metal wire between metal posts.

"Why has the goblet disappeared in France?" Barral asked rhetorically. He quickly answered, "It's because of the tractor. It is easier to use a tractor when the vines are trained flat in rows two meters apart." But the goblet is important, Barral said, because the plant forms a natural umbrella that prevents soils from baking in the southern summer sun. The shade also allows the fruit to ripen slowly and naturally and produce more acids—adding lightness and elegance. And *acidity*—nearly always lacking in hot climates like southern France or California—is to Barral more than *important*. In fact, it his holy grail in creating great, balanced wines.

Barral showed me his tractors, which were small and equipped with caterpillar tracks rather than wheels so as not to compact the soils in his vineyard. And he insisted that the tractors work the soil in two perpendicular directions.

"Look at the vines of my neighbors . . . Look what happens when the tractor goes in one direction—it creates ravines and all the soil washes away. Look at my vines—there is not one ravine." Barral was right, the soil in his vines was level and intact, whereas his neighbors' vineyards tended to have areas that were washed out and eroded, and some had developed large pools of standing water in the tracks of tractor tires.

On the Faugerès landscape there was another difference in Barral's vines: though the vines were brown and dormant, the land was green. Barral counted weeds as part of the biodiversity, an appreciation that many of his neighbors did not share.

"You can count thirty-nine different varieties of weeds in the vines," Barral said, again on his haunches, peeling back a handful of prairie grass at the base of one of his vines. Barral ran his fingers delicately through the soil, handling small pieces of wood, a large earth worm, and decaying roots. "You see, it's not compacted at all," Barral said. "This is all decomposing matter. *Très, très, très important, tout ça.*"

At one point we came upon a small group of workers who were trimming back vines in Barral's vineyards and talking among themselves at the same time. All five of them were women. "We work with a lot of girls," Barral said. "French, Portuguese, Spanish."

"That's *important* too?" I asked.

"*Oui!*" he said. "Women pay more attention when they cut. They are more careful. *Très important.*"

At morning's end we returned to Barral's collection of buildings and barns that straddle the only road that goes through Lenthéric. Vehicles seldom passed. The air had a light cedar smell, and the only sounds from downtown Lenthèric came from Barral's chickens and pigeons in the coop in front of his home, from his small children running about, and from the winter birds lighting in the plane trees.

Important to Barral's winemaking are techniques as rustic as his agriculture. Wines are not filtered: his white wine—made principally from local terret blanc—appears as cloudy as apple cider until a layer of sediment settles in the bottom of the bottle. He rarely adds sulfites. Most of the grapes used in making his three cuvées of red wine—from carignan, grenache, cinsault, syrah, and mourvèdre— are not destemmed. Overhanging his whole winemaking operation were some cobwebs made by what must have been some very large spiders—no doubt *très important* to the operation as well.

Barral led me through a barn door and into one of the buildings where he aged his wines in standard reused Bordeaux barriques. We tasted our way across the room and yet another, Barral withdrawing barrel samples with a pipette. At one point Barral paused in front of two barrels to make a point.

The first barrel contained carignan from 2004 in which none of the grapes had been destemmed. The second was syrah from the same year in which only half the grapes had been destemmed. Both of these would be included in a final blend that wouldn't make it to the market until 2008.

The wines couldn't have been more different. The first had a light refreshing acidity. The second was big and tannic and seemed to lack acidity.

"It's bizarre," Barral said, "the stems are supposed to make wine bigger, but I'm finding that when the stems are ripe they make the wine actually taste more acidic and balanced! I had an analysis done on these two barrels and they have identical acidity—there is no difference in the analysis."

"So where does that freshness come from?" Barral asked himself, evidently not for the first time. "It must come from something else . . . some molecule . . ."

I left Barral to ponder the mysteries of acidity and wine chemistry. I was headed off to explore the effects of a potentially more powerful force: celebrity.

My next destination was Aniane, about an hour northeast of Faugères. Aniane is a typically worn Languedoc village that in winter turns a sad shade of monotone grey. Yet just outside the village confines, Aniane is surrounded by vibrant red and ochre rocky landscapes, dense forests, and ancient relics that attract legions of summer tourists, hikers, and all-terrain cyclists. A few miles outside the town—perched on a gorge above the Herault River—drinkable spring water runs out of the fountains and down through the streets and past art galleries and glass blowers in postcard-perfect Saint-Guilhem-le-Désert, built around a twelfth-century abbey.

In the wine world Aniane is distinguished by a confluence of singular events. The first was the luck of prehistoric geology that gave the region's hills its soils loaded with ancient river rock, red glacial deposits, limestone, and sand.

The second event was the arrival in 1971 of Aimé Guibert, the former leather goods manufacturer, who with his wife, Veronique, bought an old flour mill in the Gassac Valley. After a famed Bordeaux geography professor, Henri Enjalbert, came to study the land and concluded it was a terroir on the order of the finest of Bordeaux or Burgundy, the Guiberts set about planting dozens of vineyards— mostly cabernet sauvignon—tucked into the forested hillsides. Shunning chemicals and using only cuttings from noncloned antique vines, Mas de Daumas Gassac became the precursor of natural wines and the quality movement in Languedoc as well as one of the priciest table wines in the world. (The winery's emphasis on cabernet and a dozen other nonlocal varietals from around the winegrowing world precluded it from being classified as part of the Coteaux-du-Languedoc when the appellation was created in 1985.)

The third event of note came in the year 2000 when locals learned that the socialist mayor and city council planned to lease 123 acres of high forest land to American winemaker Robert Mondavi, who planned to invest millions replacing the forest with vineyards to make $60-a-bottle syrah. The upshot of L'Affaire Mondavi, documented in the movie *Mondovino* (2004), was that the locals booted out the mayor in 2001, voting for his communist rival, who stopped the deal in its tracks.

The fourth event came in 2003 when French film star Gerard Depardieu and his partner, the international wine dealer Bernard Magrez, bought about six acres of vineyards outside Aniane to add to their stable of expensive garage-style wines, aided by wine consultant and *Mondovino* villain Michel Rolland.

Depardieu's presence in Aniane seems to have been greeted by reactions varying from irritation to indifference. Winemakers complained how Depardieu's purchase had doubled the price of vineyard lands, and questioned the red carpet that seemed to be awaiting the actor at Aniane's city hall. (The new mayor was quoted in a local newspaper as saying that he had personally cooked a wild pig for Depardieu and found the actor thoroughly charming.) I met no one in Aniane who had tasted Depardieu's first wine effort in 2003, which he called "Le Bien Décidé" (the resolute)—or at least anyone who would admit to it.

I had come to Aniane to visit Depardieu's wine neighbors, the husband-and-wife team of Jean-Pierre and Isabelle Venture. The Ventures established their tidy modern winery called Mas de la Seranne in 1998—returning to Isabelle's ancestral home and buying up twelve acres and later another twenty-two—after Jean-Pierre quit his job as industrial engineer and cake plant manager for Pillsbury.

"It was our way of rediscovering the land of our ancestors," Jean-Pierre said on this bright morning. He was a man bristling with energy at midlife, his personality barely contained under his sunbaked, wide-brimmed hat.

In seven years, the Ventures had built a going concern and were not having a problem selling their wine—some 90 percent of which was sold in France, with the remaining 10 percent exported to

Switzerland and Belgium. They also had succeeded in creating a local sub-appellation known as the Terrasses du Larzac.

Walking around those terraces facing the Seranne Mountains, Jean-Pierre proudly pointed out varied soils: yellow sandy loam, round river rocks, and small limestone pebbles. The Ventures did not use herbicides and practiced *lutte raisonné* (treating with reason), meaning that they treated only when they believed it was needed and not systematically. When I mentioned Barral's name, Jean-Pierre laughed and said, "He's crazy—an extremist."

The Ventures were, however, as close to their vines as Barral was to his, even though they did not share the same approach. Where Barral's vines were groomed to hang loose in all directions, the Ventures' vines were trained with military precision on uniformly taut metal wires. The younger vines were planted with the two arms of the trunk crossed—a technique, he said, that gave them more strength and insured that the grape bunches jutted forward toward the sun without touching each other.

Jean-Pierre pointed to a hillside known as Les Brousses, where Mas de la Seranne produced its prestige cuvée "Antonin et Louis" in a small vineyard that had once belonged to Isabelle's great-uncle. We then hopped in Jean-Pierre's Jeep and drove up there.

At Les Brousses the Ventures owned two acres, next to Depardieu's land: the same elevation, the same limestone pebble soil, the same dominance of syrah and carignan vines, the same southern exposure. As we drove closer to his famous neighbor's vines, Jean-Pierre scoffed, "Of course, his are not the best vines in the sector."

"Why do you say that?" I asked.

"Look, they are somewhat in a goblet . . . somewhat trained on wire—that's not good. It's better to either have a goblet that's good and open or to support the vines on the wire so the grapes don't touch. Otherwise there is a risk of rot."

In an adjacent plot, Venture's wife was among the vines, wearing leather gloves and a broad smile as she carefully trimmed the plants with a couple of workers. On that day there was no one in Depardieu's vineyard to nurture the vines of the one-time middle-school dropout and juvenile delinquent turned *artiste*. Next to the

Ventures' mothered plots, Depardieu's vineyard looked like a neglected bachelor pad. The face of French cinema, I thought, was probably off eating truffles hundreds of miles away, or giving press interviews on the other side of the globe.

"Depardieu put his picture on the bottle and he sells it for thirty-eight euros!" Venture said. "It's the same *terroir* as ours; we sell it for seventeen euros. Is the wine twice as good? Or is it the label?"

I asked Venture what he thought of Depardieu's wine.

"I've never tasted it."

Before I left town, I stopped by the Aniane wine cooperative, with which Depardieu Inc. had struck an accord to sell his wine. I bought a bottle of Le Bien Décidé 2003—served in a tall, hefty bottle with an extra-long phallic neck and an unsmiling watercolor portrait of the artist on the back.

The following Saturday I was back at home—one of those hard-raining days in our patch of countryside, where you can stay in and watch the floodwaters rise in the stream next to the house or invite friends over to eat and drink.

At noon I opened three bottles in the cellar: Le Mas de la Seranne's Antonin et Louis 2003, Depardieu's effort from the same year, and Barral's Jadis 2002. I wrapped the bottles in aluminum foil for the sport of hiding their identities.

At five we descended to the cellar with a sausage, bread, and glasses. My tasting friends included Philippe, a natural "nose" as a Frenchman who worked for a large scents manufacturer near Grasse and sold *aromes* for everything from perfume to chewing gum to cuisine around the world; Ken, an American software engineer who in his younger days had studied winemaking in Alsace and later worked for Mondavi's Opus One in California; and Daniel, who had grown up among his father's vines in Alsace after the war.

I first served the Mas de la Seranne, which produced lots of approving noises such as "hmmmm" . . . "good fruit" . . . "licorice scents" . . . "refined" . . . "velvety." All three of my guests guessed this was a Rhône Valley wine. Perhaps, Ken ventured, it was a northern Rhône like Côte Rôtie. He nailed the alcohol level at 14 percent.

Next up was the Depardieu wine.

"Oh my God!" Philippe exclaimed, screwing up his face in disgust at his first sip. "This is not wine; it is a port or vermouth. It's for an aperitif. For someone who likes . . . whiskey."

I couldn't resist asking what famous person it reminded him of. "Fidel Castro!"

"Wow, it's a dragster," Ken said, again accurately pegging the alcohol content. "At least 15 percent alcohol . . . It reminds me of some California zinfandels."

"I agree," Philippe opined. "It's not a French wine. A New World wine. Maybe from South Africa."

Then came the Barral wine.

"*Classique*," Daniel said.

"*Classique*," Ken echoed. "French, maybe Italian . . . dry."

"Hugo Chavez!" Philippe exclaimed, allowing that it could be the residue of the second wine (the Depardieu creation) that had him stuck on Latin American dictators.

After I unwrapped the bottles, the discussion restarted, particularly over Depardieu's wine. We all agreed it was the kind of big, bombastic, heavy-breathing wine you'd expect from Depardieu, who in France had become synonymous with his roles in the comic-book-inspired *Asterix* films as Obelisk, the rotund Roman-era Gaul with pigtails and an unending appetite.

On the front of the bottle, a charcoal-gray diamond-shaped label announced the name of the wine and Aniane in copper metallic letters. Below that was:

Gérard Depardieu
Acteur
Propriétaire de vignobles

It was odd that he had chosen to identify himself first as *acteur*. Months earlier, after a string of flops at the domestic box office, Depardieu had dramatically announced on a movie set his forthcoming retirement from the cinema ("I have nothing left to prove"). The fifty-six-year-old actor said he would spend his time in his far-flung vineyards.

It was also odd that after the wine's identity was revealed, I noticed the ever-so-slight backtracking by Philippe in his feelings about it.

"Of course all the wines are very good . . . ," he said, adding how the Depardieu wine showed that France can produce New World–style wines. "That is a wine I would love to give to my father," he went on. "He hates Depardieu, but this is exactly the kind of wine he would like."

Was Philippe starstruck? Had a nerve of Gallic pride been touched? Or perhaps some unresolved oedipal conflict had surfaced. In a matter of minutes he'd gone from nearly spitting the stuff out to wanting to give it to his dad.

Is there any potable liquid so psychologically charged? What neurons spin around in the brain in anticipation at the sight of the label? The French wine industry is expert in this field: supermarket shelves are crowded with knockoff names and labels that transparently mimic all the grandeur of the grands crus. If faith can transform table wine into a sacrament, can't marketing turn ordinary "La Feet" into Château Lafite or perhaps a more modest Lafitte or decent Laffitte? How did a generation of American hip-hop musicians get hooked on Louis Roederer's Cristal Champagne? Was it the finesse of the bubbles and subtle fruit aromas that impressed P. Diddy and 50 Cent? Or was it the gold bling label and the price tag over $200 that says *serious candidates only*? (In 2006 Roederer's managing director expressed concern about the impact on his brand in an interview in *The Economist*. Rapper Jay-Z, crying "racism," led a boycott of Cristal in favor of other pricey champagnes such as Dom Pérignon and Krug.)

I remembered leaving Didier Barral, happily immersed in his vines and animal excrement in Lenthèric. I'd told him that I was going to Aniane, wanting to get his impression of Depardieu—the *propriétaire de vignobles*.

"But that's not wine," Barral had said. "It has *nothing to do* with wine."

"No?" I'd wondered. "What is it then?"

Barral didn't have to think about it: "C'est le showbiz."

The Soul of Côte Rôtie

DRIVING NORTH UP THE MOTORWAY along the Rhône Valley, the whole world seemed to change at Valence. It had started as a crisp cloudless January morning in Provence as I tooled up the highway through the winter-bare vineyards of the south, such as Côtes-du-Luberon, Gigondas, and Châteauneuf-du-Pape. Neil Young was whining away on the car stereo; there was nothing but big blue skies and open road ahead. Hardly anyone seemed to be going in my direction.

Then just after Valence, I understood why. Heavy gray fog sat at treetop level and grew thicker with every fraction of a mile. The sky, which a few instants earlier had seemed limitless, shrunk into a patch of blue in my rearview mirror and then disappeared. In about five minutes the dashboard thermometer reading dropped from 11°C (52°F) to 4°C (39°F). As I climbed up the northern Rhône Valley, I felt as though I'd left the south of France and entered what could have been a suburb of Frankfurt.

Had I been able to see anything more than a few meters of pavement ahead, I might have appreciated that I was passing some of France's great northern Rhône appellations such as Cornas and Hermitage. But I could not. By the time I reached my destination, a light, cold rain was falling on the village of Ampuis.

Not much goes on in Ampuis. Route nationale 86 is the town's main drag, lined by a few bistro/bars and bakeries, the local co-op, and other small businesses. A church and a parking lot give form to what could be called the town's main square. Between the road and the river is a freight train line and an old, regal-looking Château d'Ampuis. At first glance this is Anytown, France.

9. The vineyards near Ampuis in winter

I arrived in Ampuis on a Thursday around noon, the day before the start of the annual Côte Rôtie wine market, which was being set up in the village's multipurpose hall—a basketball gymnasium with no bleachers. My first stop was the bistro across from church, where I ordered the *plat du jour*, a *Parmentier de Sanglier*, a creamy potato-and-wild-boar gratin (named for the French agriculturalist credited with introducing spuds to the French plate in the eigteenth century). No Mediterranean diet here: the area around Lyon is considered by many to be France's culinary cholesterol-pumping heart, and sanglier is always on the menu.

After lunch the sky had begun to clear, and I walked away from the nationale and up into one of the most dramatic collections of vineyards I've seen anywhere. Just a few blocks west of town, the hills rise at a pitch so steep that it's hard to imagine how anyone thought to cultivate them. Rows upon rows of vines cling to the hillsides—each vine braced against the wind and elements by a pair of two-meter wood posts bound together teepee-like at the top.

In fact, it was the Romans who planted syrah grapes in what is now known as the Côte Rôtie, or "roasted hill." The area reached its peak of production at the end of the nineteenth century with 300 hectares (about 740 acres) of wine cultivation. But then the industrial age and two world wars wiped out most of the manual labor force. By the 1950s, 80 percent of the vineyards were abandoned and the wine sold cheap. In the 1960s, dirt paths on the hillsides traveled by donkeys for millennia were replaced with the first small paved roads. The 1970s saw a new generation of winemakers take to the vineyards with an eye on the export market, and by the end of the decade a renaissance was under way.

Côte Rôtie sits at the northern growing limit of syrah, and its wines taste like no other. Exclusively red, they have a velvety finesse and staying power that is sometimes likened to fine Burgundies with the added spiciness and body lent by syrah. So it goes without saying that Côte Rôtie is no secret among the *vinoscenti*. Robert Parker, in the sixth edition of his *Wine Buyer's Guide*, called Côte Rôtie "one of France's greatest wines." The hillsides—about 540 acres are now under production—are organized into some seventy vineyard areas. A tributary that runs through Ampuis and under the highway divides two prominent slopes—the northern slope, known as Côte-Brune, and the southern Côte-Blonde. Nowadays, in a bastardized shorthand geography, everything to the south is often referred to as "Blonde"—an area known for producing lighter, more aromatic wines in beige-toned soils. Everything to the north is often referred to as "Brune"—synonymous wines that pack more punch, grown from dark, iron-rich soils laced with schist.

In all, Côte Rôtie's fifty or so winemakers produce about a million bottles of wine per year, and they don't last long. In the United States even the generic bottlings of the Côte Rôtie's one big player, negociant-producer Marcel Guigal, sold for well over $50. Guigal's prestige wines, with grapes from a single vineyard, can sell for upward of $300.

Still, apart from Guigal, who bought the turreted Château d'Ampuis and impresses his special guests there, there is little that is regal in Ampuis. Heading back to town, I passed small wineries with signs of family life—a kid's bicycle out front or a living room upstairs. Parked in front of these wineries were trucks, not Bentleys. They were owned by people—I would come to learn—who, like in any sleepy rural town, tend not only to know each other very well but also to know each other's business.

Next to the bistro where I had lunch was the bed-and-breakfast in which I would be spending the next two nights. It was run by Gilles Barge, a fifth-generation family winemaker who, with his wife, rented out serviceable rooms above their home on the square.

Barge, then forty-eight years old with a long ruddy face and what struck me as a genuine smile, agreed to give me a tour of his nearby winery. He wore jeans, running shoes, and a black leather hat rimmed with crocodile teeth (a souvenir of a trip to Australia). We climbed into his truck for the two-minute commute.

We entered the winery through a garage door below the apartment where his parents live, and walked through a doorway into a long, chilly room that had been the kitchen of his great-grandfather. Barge set about making a fire in the large fireplace, saying that we would return here after the room heated up.

Among Côte Rôtie producers, Barge, who served as president of the local winemakers' association for twelve years ending in 2002, is known as a leader of the traditionalist camp—in opposition to modernists such as Guigal and others who make more superconcentrated, powerful Côte Rôties.

"The wine of Côte Rôtie is not the same as it was a hundred years ago, and it is even less like it was two thousand years ago,"

Barge said, with a note of regret in his voice. "The tastes of people have changed."

Barge is such a stickler for tradition that up until the tough harvest of 2002—a wet year in which winegrowers were forced to pick their grapes early—he'd refused to de-stem his grapes. Generally speaking, leaving the stems on makes a more rustic, age-worthy wine with lots of natural tannins, but it means that wines are more difficult to drink in their youth.

During fermentation and its immediate aftermath before pressing, most winemakers punch down, stomp, or mechanically press the *chapeau* (cap) or hard crust of skins and seeds (and stems in some cases) that forms in their wine vats; or they pump wine from the bottom of the vat over the cap. All of this is done with the intent of extracting the tannins and flavor.

It's a subtle point. But in Barge's view, such extraction techniques are a form of cheating wine, which he believes should come to be in the gentlest way possible. In his fermentation area Barge had me stick my head inside an empty steel vat. What did I see inside? he quizzed. I noticed around the perimeter of the interior, toward the top of the tank, a series of stainless steel hooks. Barge then explained that the hooks were part of a system in which he used crisscrossed steel wire to keep that floating wine crust submerged under the surface of the wine—a system that allowed for the most subtle extraction of aromas and flavors. He was proud of this design; bygone generations had used wood boards in a similar manner.

I was not completely convinced of the singular genius of Barge's system. But his general view made sense. To paraphrase, contemporary winemakers are faced with a choice between having their fermenting vats resemble the gentleness of Walden Pond or the turbulence of an automatic dishwasher. This was important, Barge insisted, because the dishwasher camp—extraction and big wines at all cost—was becoming conventional wisdom. "Côte Rôtie should not be about force and power," Barge protested. "It's about aromas and subtlety."

We then descended a set of stairs into Barge's *chais*, the cellar where wine is raised before bottling in wood barrels. Barge's chais was a typical low-ceilinged dark room with wood barrels stacked on their sides, each marked on its face in chalk indicating the type of wine and vintage inside.

In the Côte Rôtie, wines generally spend two years in the barrel before their release. But that is about all Côte Rôtie winemakers agree on when it comes to wood. At the dawn of the twenty-first century, Ampuis was consumed by a passionate battle over the use of wood, with clear lines of demarcation. Guigal as well as smaller producers, such as Barge's brother-in-law Jean-Michel Gerin, were on the advanced guard of the wood trend—aging all their wines in new-oak, Bordeaux-style barriques. Barge and the *resistants* preferred mellower, older (and often larger) barrels that they say are more subtle in their effects on the wine. They insist that new wood overwhelms the nuances.

"Toasted, vanilla, roasted," Barge said as mocked the vocabulary of flavors that fresh wood lays on wine. "I think it's sad, and to me it doesn't have anything to do with *terroir*. I've been saying it for twenty-five years: Wine should smell and taste like the variety of grapes and the place it was produced from, and that is all!"

"The best-made barrel in the world," he concluded in a flourish, "is still as stupid as a scrap of wood."

Barge pulled the cork bung out of the up-facing side of a barrel marked as 2004 Cuvée du Plessy, which he explained was produced by the Côte Blonde and other vineyards south of the Blonde-Brune line. He withdrew some wine from the barrel with a pipette and poured it into a glass.

At first taste it reminded me of the most recent great bottle of wine my wife and I had shared. It was Christmastime and we'd ordered a foie gras—a whole raw fattened duck liver, which my wife sliced and seared in a pan with mangoes. For that meal we'd shared a bottle of 2001 Côte Rôtie from the "blonde" area.

That bottle had finesse, an earthy bouquet, and "length"—meaning that I could taste it going down, all the way down the center of my tongue, down and into the place where I once had tonsils. Barge opened more barrels for tasting, but nothing else came close to that 2004—a baby wine I'd have to wait at least another two years to get my hands on.

We went back up to the upstairs ancestral kitchen where a crackling fire awaited us. On a thick wooden table sat five opened bottles that Barge had used for a group of visitors a day earlier. We went down the row tasting each one in turn. Everything from 2002—a difficult vintage that had been pilloried by the wine press—tasted thin and bitter, at least for now. A 2001 was delicious, but I couldn't get the 2004 out of my taste memory.

"Do you know what the difference between a good wine and a great wine is?" Barge gave me an intent look.

I thought for some moments, listening to the hungry fire and the air being sucked up the chimney. Great wines often pack an element of surprise, of complexity, that unfolded with every sip and every glass. Sometimes their charms were fleeting, ephemeral. Seductive, even transcendental. Great wines were surely always drunk in great company . . .

Barge interrupted my reverie. "A good wine is a wine you find to be good. A great wine is a wine that you remember."

"As for all the rest . . . All the rest is literature."

I'd arranged to meet the man who produced my Christmastime Côte Rôtie first thing Friday morning in a parking lot just off the nationale south of Ampuis. There were no signs indicating Jean-Michel Stephan's small winery in the town of Tupin-Semons (a merged name from two vine-covered "blonde" slopes), and Madame Stephan had set up our meeting point.

I arrived early and parked in one of three spaces by the side of a country road. I waited about five minutes. Then a short bespectacled man resembling Corporal "Radar" O'Reilly in the TV series *M*A*S*H* arrived across the road. He glanced at me. I looked at him. Then he looked away. He lit a cigarette. A couple of minutes later, he called out to me, "Are you waiting for someone?" Yes, I called back. And Stephan introduced himself.

It was only at this point that I matched Stephan to the face on the promotional literature I'd picked up at my local wine merchant, or *caviste*. Stephan's "brochure" was actually just one black-and-white letter-sized page that appeared to have been run off on a home printer and announced "Le Vin en Liberté" (Wine in Liberty). On the back was a pair of fuzzy images of a young *vigneron* in rumpled sweater and jeans—in one image he was among his vines holding a pair of clippers, and in the other, standing indoors with an arm around his wife.

At thirty-three years old, Stephan was the antithesis of glamour—a man who exuded shyness and social awkwardness. Incongruously, his brochure listed as venues for his wine some of the chicest restaurants on the planet: Hôtel Georges V in Paris, Marc Vérat in Megève, and Daniel in New York. It would take some effort to imagine a person who would be more out of place than Stephan in some of those tony luxury palaces.

Stephan and I walked about twenty yards to his home and winery, where winemaking machinery was crammed under a carport. We got in his battered Citroën truck and headed out to his vines.

As the first winemaker in his family, Stephan is an outsider in Côte Rôtie. His grandparents grew fruits and vegetables. His father grows apples, pears, and apricots. Stephan became fascinated with winemaking at an early age and began planting vines on a family hillside plot when he was fourteen. He went north for his winemaking studies in Beaujolais, and while doing his mandatory military service in the French army, he said, "I had a captain who liked Côte Rôtie."

The sympathetic officer arranged for Stephan to work as a waiter in a military commissary with a flexible schedule that allowed for him to travel home weekends to tend to his vines. Fresh out of the army in 1991, Stephan used his local contacts to begin collecting leases of local parcels, including some of the oldest in the Côte Rôtie.

We stepped out of his truck halfway up the last in the chain of hillsides forming the appellation. Here we stood at the southern tip of Côte Rôtie in the "blonde" area known as Coteaux de Semons. Across a small valley began the white wine hills and appellation of Condrieu.

Stephan knelt down to touch the soil. It was light and sandy and on close examination you could see that the sand was speckled with small pieces of granite. As I looked down the slope, I noticed something I hadn't noticed in any other vines in the Côte Rôtie. Throughout the appellation, the hills I'd seen were bare of any growth in winter—almost lunar-looking. Here among about two and half acres of Stephan's vines, however, were patches of undergrowth and plants growing between the rows.

"Ah, the weeds," Stephan shrugged. "My vines always have weeds."

Because of the topography of Côte Rôtie, using a tractor to turn soils is usually impossible. As a result most winegrowers use some herbicides. As part of his *vin en liberté* philosophy, Stephan used no chemicals. Sometimes he used a small gas-powered tiller to unearth his weeds, and where it wasn't possible—such as on the Coteaux de Semons—he simply left the weeds alone.

Stephan's attitude toward weeds hadn't gone unnoticed. Another young winemaker referred to Stephan's brand of agriculture as "relaxed," and he didn't mean that as a compliment. Conventional thinking among winegrowers is that weeds compete with vines for water and therefore cut grape production. Stephan acknowledged that competition from his weeds cuts his yields in half, but he didn't seem at all bothered by that. "If I get less fruit, so what?" he said. His goal was only to produce about ten thousand bottles of wine in all from about eleven acres. The rest he sold to Guigal and other negociants in the form of either grapes or wine.

The vines on this hillside were planted in 1902—some of the oldest in the Côte Rôtie. To get these small, stumpy vines to produce a reasonable amount of fruit was usually a challenge. Vine by vine, Stephan delicately bends and ties into an arc the sole fruit-bearing shoots—thus separating the grape clusters and giving each ample exposure.

Most of the rest of his vines, he said, were modern, more robust cloned varietals like nearly all of what is planted in the world: "clones," he said with a measure of deprecation. Some of his "clones" were on the plateau above the traditional Côte Rôtie. The plateau, added to the appellation in 1940, is flat and easier to cultivate by tractor. But Stephan said in some years it produces fruit that is less than fully ripe: "mediocre." "Usually, I sell those grapes to the negociants. The grapes that interest me, I keep."

We returned to Stephan's winery and entered through a garage door. Inside was a typical hangar where Stephan did his vinification in stainless steel vats. In normal years he produces three wines: his regular Côte Rôtie, a wine made just from those old vines we saw that morning, and a third made with grapes from a plot perched vertiginously above Tupin.

In 2002 he made only one wine: "Instead of making three small wines, I made one average-plus wine." Stephan opened a bottle of his 2002 and set it down on a small table that held his labeling machine. He found a pair of glasses and poured. Like the other 2002s I'd tasted, this one was "nervous"—acidic to the point of being bitter. But Stephan, like many fellow winemakers in the Côte Rôtie that year, insisted that with the passage of time the acidity would mellow and the wine would find its balance. For those who didn't want to wait to drink the wine, Stephen suggested not just letting the wine breathe, but giving it a small vacation in open air. "I tell people to open it forty-eight hours in advance."

Stephan's chais was accessible only by a wooden ladder that dropped through a hole in the floor—a challenge while balancing a wine glass. Down in his cellar among the barrels, we tasted his three cuvées from 2003, a year that had been the inverse of 2002. France's legendary heat wave of 2003 had produced sugar-rich grapes that made strong, highly alcoholic wines. In the Côte Rôtie I heard several winemakers complain that, based on the "vintage of the century" hype surrounding the 2003 vintage hundreds of miles away in Bordeaux, clients were already calling to place blind orders for a wine that was not really like a Côte Rôtie. "The wine is too strong, too hot," Stephan said. "It's like a Côte Rôtie Languedoc-style."

As Stephan withdrew samples, he described how each of his wines was made. Yet he did it in a way I'd never heard from a winemaker—delivered as though he were making a confession. Stephan held up a wine glass to the light of a hanging bulb and divulged that this wine could not be considered traditional, because he had removed the grape stems prior to fermentation.

"*Rafflage*," Stephan said using the French word for de-stemming, "is good for immediate pleasure. People don't have patience anymore—I speak of course for 90 percent of people. My fear is that one day we aren't going to have wines to keep from the old vintages."

For his old-vines bottling, which tasted longer in the mouth and more complex than his basic wine, Stephan said he also de-stemmed the grapes and then cracked the grape skins before fermentation. For both wines he used a form of manual *pigeage*—meaning that he broke up the wine cap and immersed it in the wine the popular old-fashioned way: he opened up the vats from the top and stomped on the caps in his bare feet.

In the world of wine, Stephan's techniques were hardly sins. But he seemed ready to argue all day that doing just about anything other than putting grape clusters in a vat and letting them ferment was a shortcut. "*Rafflage, pigeage*," he rhymed, "it's all a form of *dopage* (doping)."

Stephan considered himself apart from the two main camps of Côte Rôtie traditionalists versus modernists. His was a third way of small-production, innovative, natural winemakers who recognized tradition but were not bound by it. He and others like him rejected chemicals, additives, and other tricks of technology. Not only were his wines unfiltered, he also took the rare—some would say extreme—risk of not dosing his wine with sulfur (referred to on wine labels as "sulfites"). Because sulfur kills off bacteria and yeasts and acts as a preservative against spoiling, very few winemakers are willing to do without it, particularly at bottling time. (Nonsulfured wines need to be kept cool—under 60°F.)

The wine Stephan considered his purest—his true *vin en liberté*—was his third wine, the Coteaux Tupin, made with carbonic maceration. While it sounds like something used to make Coca-Cola rather than Côte Rôtie, it is a style of fermentation common in Beaujolais. Stephan insisted it was a technique *les anciennes* (past generations) would have approved of—had it been available. With *carbonique*, a vat is filled with carbon dioxide (a naturally occurring product of fermentation), grape clusters are dropped in, and voilà . . . the rest is left to nature. Deprived of oxygen, the grapes ferment slowly, from the inside out, resulting in lighter but aromatic red wines.

Stephan used a popular *Franglais* term to describe the process: "C'est soft." However, after fermentation the wine was raised two years in not very "soft" new oak barrels, which Stephan justified by saying, "Oak was used in the Middle Ages." "I do nothing," Stephan proclaimed triumphantly, looking me in the eye. "It's a wine sans intervention."

Stephan's "soft" 2003 smelled of spicy licorice, and it tasted mellower than the typically tannic and brash 2003s of Côte Rôtie. The overall feel was silky, elegant. And though it was still not fully formed, it was a wine I would recall long after that day—a wine I would track down more two winters later (after all of Stephan's stock disappeared) and savor with friends until all that was left was the bottle (labeled with a child's white-on-black finger painting) and the fine drops of memory.

After finishing the morning in Stephan's cellar, I spent part of the afternoon just up the road, but in a place that couldn't have been any further away: a place where man's intervention—particularly the intervention of one man who produces some six million bottles of wine annually in all the Rhône Valley—is not lamented but celebrated.

From the outside, the Guigal winery is a large, well-kept block of a plant on the edge of Ampuis. I walked off the street through a pair of automatic sliding glass doors and into a reception area where I was blinded by the glint of chrome and the sheen of deep squared-off modern sofas covered in top-grain red leather.

I announced my presence and my appointment for a tour of the winery to a secretary, who I assumed—after the reception I'd so far received in Ampuis—would just ring Monsieur Guigal ("Call me Marcel," he would of course insist) and off we'd go for a visit to the cellars and then up the road to the old château.

As I waited, I picked up a gold-embossed, beautifully designed color brochure. On the cover was a sprawling image of the Château d'Ampuis along the banks of the Rhône. The inside opened with a pair of winged dragons supporting a coat of arms. On the back cover there was an image of a treasure chest labeled "the treasures of Domaine Guigal," which you peeled open to reveal small cards detailing each of Guigal's prestige cuvées. And inside on one semitransparent page of text was a quote from Sir Francis Bacon: "We cannot command nature except by obeying her." The overall impression was of power, prestige, and profundity.

I quickly learned I would get to visit the cellar, but there was no mention of Monsieur Guigal. Instead, I was attached to a visiting group of about twenty-five women from Avignon accompanied by their local wine merchant. Our guide was an earnest young man who looked to be about twenty. He had a head thick with black curls and wore narrow black pants and a black turtleneck.

I joined the group in one of the dark and damp old vaulted sub-terranean passageways where Guigal ages hundreds of thousands of liters of wine in new wood barriques. The walls were thick with naturally occurring molds and little decorative touches: in a small niche a spotlight illuminated a dripping fountain with a small cherub holding a bunch of grapes.

Guigal, we were told, employs a full-time barrel maker just to make the oak casks that would hold Guigal prestige wines for some forty-two months before release. The young man explained that Monsieur Guigal himself personally goes walking through certain oak forests of Burgundy to select the trees fortunate enough to be felled for his barrels. I could sense a collective swoon of appreciation from the ladies of Avignon. After their use, our guide explained offhandedly, these barriques were sold to small producers in town who could not afford new wood. The ladies now believed that everyone would certainly want to use new wood, and that Monsieur Guigal (was it caring for the little winemakers or was it smart business acumen?) had found a way to recycle his gently used handcrafted goods.

No apologies for modernity here. Everything, we were told, was state-of-the-art: de-stemming machines, temperature controls, the turbines and pumps in the steel tanks that aided the extraction process for these prized wines. While Guigal was just now putting out his 2001 wines, we were told that the most prestigious cuvées would not be released until the great American wine critic Robert Parker had published his reviews—only then could prices be set for the international market.

Meanwhile, in my head I was doing simple math. It struck me as incredible that Guigal, with only about 110 acres of his own—just 10 times the amount that Stephan was cultivating—could produce 600 times the amount of wine through his business dealings buying grapes and wine as a negociant.

Our young guide assured us that Guigal buys only the best grapes from local producers, and I thought of Stephan—a Guigal supplier— out among his weeds, saying that his best grapes are kept for bottles that bear his own name.

At the end of nearly an hour-long tour, we were led to a tasting area in the cellar surrounded by large casks holding the latest Guigal crus from his single-vineyard Côte Rôtie wines. Our young guide set out glasses on a massive round bar. The Avignon ladies snapped photos.

The Côte Rôtie portion of this tasting would consist of two cuvées from the 2001 vintage: Guigal's "Brune et Blonde" (deceptively named because it contains wine from all over the Côte Rôtie and not just the two vineyards as it implies) and Château d'Ampuis.

The first wine was perfectly acceptable—no flaws but not inspiring either. The second one was richer and more nuanced. Perhaps the only default is that it would end up with a price tag way over my budget at twice the price of a typical Côte Rôtie. I can't say I found the wood overbearing. But was this—as the wine establishment would have us believe—any more complex, aromatic, or delicious than many bottles of Côte Rôtie that sell for a fraction of the price?

I am sure that up at the château itself, lunching with Monsieur Guigal, the stuff tastes like it's worth every centime.

On Friday afternoon the streets of Ampuis were a symphony of sirens. The most shocking crime in years was unfolding. That morning, a fifty-five-year-old man diagnosed with terminal cancer fatally shot his wife, mother-in-law, and son before calling police and taking his own life in his car in a woods near town. The man, a delivery driver, was well known among locals.

"He was sick, yes, but who could have expected this?" the woman at the wine supply cooperative gasped, shaking her head. "Besides, he even bought his ticket in advance for the wine market."

The market opened that afternoon with all the spit and polish you'd expect from, say, a high school science fair. In the lobby of the city's multipurpose hall, you paid eight euros and received a ticket and a tasting glass.

Inside the hall, simple, identical bar/stands were laid out for fifty-seven wine producers. In between them were industrial-sized spittoons fashioned from large plastic trash cans and funnel-type lids. Barge, I noticed, had lost his crocodile hunter hat and wore a maroon blazer with a dark shirt and tie. Stephan had shown up late and—like most of the vignerons—made no attempt at nattiness. The Guigal stand was abundantly staffed with men and women in dark suits and turtlenecks.

By five the place was filled with the first hundreds of wine pilgrims among thousands who would arrive over the next few days. They were typically male, French, about fifty years old, in groups of two to four. Most appeared to be at least partially balding and wore a leather parka that covered a paunch. By seven the spittoons were going unused, and the mood of the crowd was getting merry.

I ate dinner that evening at Le Cercle des Vignerons, one of my favorite wine bar/restaurant/wine stores anywhere that sells local and Rhône wines at producer prices and that has dried sausages hanging above the bar for patrons to squeeze test before buying.

At some point I fell into conversation with a couple of guys standing at the zinc bar, making a meal of *charcuterie* and a decanted bottle of Côte Rôtie. The men were both in their thirties; the taller of the two was from Lyon, the shorter one from Paris. They explained they were long-time friends who had worked the vendanges together and knew Côte Rôtie well.

The taller man offered me a glass from his decanter and showed me the bottle: 2000 Côte Rôtie—Les Rochains from Patrick and

Christophe Bonnefond. The glasses themselves were big, opulent, angular crystal—about four times as large as the standard tasting glass prescribed by France's INAO.

"Parker," the taller man editorialized, "is in my opinion a man with exceptional ability . . . But he is just one man. Parker didn't like the 2000. I don't care, I like the 2000."

From wine, the talk drifted off into the state of affairs in the world and, in particular, France. I had heard all the gripes so many times before I couldn't begin to count: crime, the indiscipline of the French, the country's growing poor Muslim population, the bureaucracy that punishes small entrepreneurs and initiative.

"What can you do?" my new friend from Lyon went on. "One must appreciate the wine and that's all, because there are big problems on the way."

He stuck his nose inside his glass, closed his eyes, and smiled. "Parker didn't like the 2000," he repeated. "I like the 2000."

I said that I liked it too and I suggested that all of France's problems were reparable. My new drinking buddies chuckled, snickered.

"Of course. Of course. But in France we think too much," Monsieur Lyon continued. "For example, what is two plus two?"

"Four," I answered.

"Yes," he smiled, "that is *chez les Anglo Saxons*. But *in France* what is two plus two?"

He saw that I didn't have an immediate response.

"In France two plus two is four . . . *approximately*!" He held up the hand not holding his wineglass and rotated it from side to side for emphasis. "It is four but not *exactly* . . . you see, there are other things to consider . . ."

"What can one do?" I said, imitating a fatalistic Frenchman.

"Exactly," Monsieur Lyon said, lifting his glass. "Exactly!"

NINE

Remembering Gaillac

Of all the vines I've seen, heard about, or whose fruit I've tasted, the forgetting vine holds a special place in my heart. This amazes me, especially when I consider that the forgetting vine doesn't exist. Not really, anyway.

I'll explain.

Gaillac is the natural home of the forgetting vine, or precisely *La Vigne de l'Oubli*, because Gaillac itself was nearly forgotten in the attic of the twentieth century. In better times for Gaillac wine—the glory days of the thirteenth century, under the jurisdiction of local Benedictine monks and the counts of Toulouse in southwest France—Gaillac became one of France's first appellations, exporting wines to northern Europe, among them a bubbly white wine produced centuries before another Benedictine in the north of France, Dom Pérignon, was credited with "inventing" what came to be known as champagne.

Then, at the birth of France's Third Republic in the 1870s, the deadly American plant aphid phylloxera lay waste to the vines of France and southern Europe. And that was when the forgetting started. Vineyards were dug up and replanted with new, highly productive clones from elsewhere that produced seas of *vin ordinaire* indistinguishable from wines from anywhere else in the southern half of France. Still today, Gaillac does produce some wonders in the form of astoundingly varied wines with one of the oddest collections of regional grapes. And that's where the forgetting vine comes in.

I drove to Gaillac with my wife and son and friends whose family

10. Robert Plageoles demonstrates the concept of the "mother leaf"

tree is rooted in southwest France. The town of Gaillac was built in red brick in the Middle Ages around a Benedictine abbey on the Tarn River. It lies on the eastern flank of what is considered the southwest—a land forged by centuries of regional wars and crusades that have since been replaced by competition among some of the world's most avid rugby clubs.

We arrived on the Thursday of the Feast of Ascension (2006)— meticulously marked every May in France not because of its significance as the day that Christ was said to have ascended to his home in heaven, but because it provides the opportunity for a four-day weekend with some of the first reliably mild weather of spring.

It was officially billed as a festive wine-filled weekend, "Springtime in Gaillac." And it showcased the Gaillac region's confused identity, which pulls from all points of the compass. That first evening we walked through the near-deserted street of the old town by the river—made from disintegrating bricks, wood timbers, and masonry. In the modern center of town, we followed a trail of hefty bovine droppings—the day's remnants of a Spanish-style "running of the bulls"—to a sprawling parking lot under the large platanes in front of the city hall. There were about a couple of hundred of Gaillacois (from the local population of 11,000), many who seemed to wear the blank, forgotten look of a countryside that has produced little culture or economic growth.

We watched a demonstration of Camargue horse riding accompanied by music from that region in coastal Provence. Then we sat shoulder-to-shoulder at plank tables and ate southwestern *confit de canard* (duck confit) and fried potatoes on paper plates. The one truly Gaillac part of the evening—the wine that flowed from the faucets of large containers into plastic cups—was free-flowing, cheap, and worth forgetting.

Friday morning, while the rest of our group was sleeping, I headed out across the countryside—where vines share space with peach and apple orchards and fields of wheat and where at 8:30 a.m. only winegrowers, roosters, and jackrabbits seemed to be awake. My destination was Domaine d'Escausses outside the tiny village of Sainte-Croix: the nest of the forgetting vine. There, I met Jean-Marc Balaran whose winery is built around his family's ancestral farmhouse looking south and west over vine-and wheat-draped hills.

Balaran was a large man of forty-eight. He wore jeans and a loose sweater, thick-rimmed eyeglasses, and an air of rare, unassuming humility.

"We have a lot of *cepages* [grape varietals], different *terroirs*, and different ideas," he said. "If you ask, 'What is a Gaillac?' I think that no one can really say."

Balaran is part of small group of Gaillac winemakers who in the last few decades have pursued a return to quality in wines made from local grape varieties. Reds can display large fruit and tannins—mixing local varietals like braucol and duras with more common syrah and cabernet sauvignon. White wines—soft and dry or late-harvest, sumptuous, honey-like nectars—are typically made from *l'oin de l'oeil* (literally "far from the eye," meaning the vine produces grapes far from its primary shoot), also called *len de l'elh*, and a family of mauzacs found throughout the southwest.

With thoroughly plainspoken openness, Balaran described his family's history, noting that the house belonged to his grandmother and that the cultivation of wine grapes and wheat goes back at least seven generations—before that no one kept track.

"There is not a history because peasants don't have history or genealogy," Balaran said. "The family has always been here."

We stood in an outbuilding that houses his wine-tasting room and boutique, the walls displaying some of the accolades and ego-pumping articles in the French wine press about Balaran and Domaine d'Escausses's ten wines.

Though he built up his family winemaking operation in the last twenty-seven years, quadrupled the Balaran vineyards to nearly one hundred acres, and achieved an enviable reputation throughout Europe and Japan, Balaran seems almost embarrassed by the attention. One French magazine recounted how, at the age of twenty-one, Balaran could have just as easily become a priest as a winemaker. "Well, that's a bit of an exaggeration," Balaran shrugged. "You know journalists; they have to make a story."

It is true, he said, that at twenty-one his life could have turned in a number of directions. After lycée, he studied business management, not wine. His daughter, Aurelie, now twenty-four, was the first generation of Balarans to receive formal training in oenology. "Making wine is like riding a bicycle," he said. "When you want to learn, you learn."

When I asked Balaran about his grape-growing methods, he mentioned the term lutte raisonée but was quick to add that the term "doesn't mean anything . . . *Tout le monde a raison*." Indeed, everybody thinks *they* are right and reasonable. The debate over the particulars of winemaking methods wasn't raging here as it was in the Côte Rôtie. Gaillac wines in general were not as coveted. Winemakers weren't writing treatises or waiting on anyone's tasting notes to set their prices. The good wines like Balaran's (a nonideological mix of tradition and modernism) were, however, a bargain. In the spring of 2006, the prices of Balaran's wines topped out at 8 euros (about US $10 at the time—though they sold for three to five times that in London).

Most winegrowers in Gaillac were just trying to get by. Balaran said the wine crisis had hurt the majority of growers in Gaillac who sold their grapes or wine in bulk to middlemen. Less affected were he and the twenty or so winemakers who focused on quality estate bottling and direct sales. Though it represented little financial gain, Balaran still cultivated about seventy-seven acres of wheat.

Expecting nothing short of a profound response, I asked Balaran about the forgetting vine. La Vigne de l'Oubli is a white wine Balaran crafts with wood-raised sauvignon blanc, muscadelle, and mauzac. It and Balaran's other wines were the first wines from Gaillac that I began to appreciate one fall with the first chill of winter air, for Balaran's wines are not to be taken lightly. They are not, as the French say, *vins d'été* (summer wines), the kind of breezy wines you chill and serve like lemonade on a hot afternoon.

La Vigne de l'Oubli is dry, nutty, and robust, and—not insignificantly—it bears a name dripping with irony and scented with a suggestion of tragedy. I wondered what exactly was forgotten. Who did the forgetting? Balaran grinned and explained that the name was not created to signify anything. It was, he said, "le marketing." A sommelier friend, Balaran explained, came up with the name to make the wine stand out on restaurant wine lists. And Gaillac wines, he went on, needed to do something to attract attention: "If you arrive in Germany or England, Gaillac is not a known label."

My first impulse was disappointment. Indignation followed. Why not just call it "Le Marketing"? But then, I figured, perhaps it was even more fitting that the forgetting vine was created—just like that—with a random firing of a brain neuron.

Yet the story of forgetting and remembrance in Gaillac does not end here. The richness and future of Gaillac, Balaran said, lay in an assortment of grape varietals found in few other places or nowhere else, including once-forgotten varieties that were now being replanted. And for the only time that morning, Balaran's voice became reverent as he spoke of a local, one-man institution who also happened to be a winemaker.

Winemaker, that is, as well as poet, painter, author, photographer, historian, book collector, antique wine grape conservationist, and raconteur, Robert Plageoles is known as the man who saved a piece of Gaillac by resurrecting the area's lost grape varieties and sharing his peripatetic experiments with fellow vignerons and the world.

At seventy-one, Robert Plageoles was more or less retired, having passed the daily operation of the two wine domains under the banner of *Les vins de Robert et Bernard Plageoles vignerons* to his fifty-year-old son, Bernard, and Bernard's wife, Myriam, while he deepened his knowledge of Gaillac and researched books like the coffee-table volume he coauthored in 2000, *Le vin de Gaillac: 2000 ans d'histoire* (Gaillac wine: 2000 years of history).

Bernard lives in the farmhouse connected to his family's ancestral Domaine des Tres Cantous just off the road that leads north from Gaillac toward the magnificent perched and fortified village of Cordes-sur-Ciel. I found Bernard alone in the morning, stacking wine bottles in cases in the winery. A group of starlings, which had built nests in the rafters, flew just over our heads.

Built like a rugby forward, with longish graying hair and an easy smile, Bernard is the fifth generation of winemaking Plageoleses— yet the first generation to formally study winemaking. In his early twenties he left Gaillac and did odd jobs as a professional driver and as a restorer of old documents—anything but winemaking— before returning to join his father in the vines.

Bernard walked me to a place across a small dirt road to a patch of land of some two hundred vines grafted and planted around 1960 by his grandfather Marcel, who collected antique varietals when he found them in the vineyards. These particular vines produced an obscure, light-golden grape known as ondenc, which had all but disappeared from Gaillac. "My grandfather knew that one day they would serve something," Bernard said, "though he didn't know what."

After Marcel's death, Bernard's father, Robert, began inquiring about this forgotten grape: "Everybody told him it wasn't great, they said the plants were fragile, that they weren't worth it." But then Robert Plageoles discovered a bit of information that would change his life and the wine of Gaillac. It came in the form of a leather-bound 1909 edition entitled *Traité pratique de préparation des vins de luxe* (*Practical Summary for Preparing Luxury Wines*) by Victor Sebastian. The book states that ondenc is susceptible to *pourriture noble*, the "noble rot" or botrytis that attacks grapes used to make the world's most renowned naturally sweet white wines. By way of comparison, Sebastian then mentioned in the same sentence the legendary Sauternes: the Château Yquem.

The father and son began experimenting with the grapes from the vines Marcel had left them—and with astounding results. The wines produced were high in sugar and alcohol, and when vinified after the onset of botrytis, they lived up to Sebastian's praise. In the early 1980s the men planted more than six acres. In recent years their sweet, golden wine known as Vin d'Autan was selected for a Hachette book in France: *Dream Bottles: The Best Wines of the World*. A handful of other Gaillac winemakers like Balaran have followed suit, planting ondenc vines.

After the ondenc experiments, Robert Plageoles became obsessed. Ondenc was like a grail that had lain right under his nose, and once he'd unearthed it, he began searching for more keys to Gaillac's past wine glories. He discovered another Gaillac antique varietal called prunelart, a stout red grape mentioned on a list of classic varietals in the French kingdom in Olivier de Serres's *Le théâtre d'agriculture*, published in 1600.

He found samples at the French state grape conservatory on the coast near Sète and set about grafting and growing prunelart in the early 1990s. Prunelart was followed by mauzac noire, another dark red varietal, and that was followed by verdanel, a white wine grape.

At the same time, the Plageoleses continued on as one of the few producers of two traditional wines produced in Gaillac: a rustic white sparkling wine as well as a *vin de voile*—a nutty, dry, deep-colored white wine that is barrel-oxidized for seven years under a veil of yeast, similar to the *vin jaune* of the Jura on the opposite side of France near Switzerland and the fortified Andalusian sherries such as Amontillado.

The Plageoleses' winemaking and growing methods are decidedly low-tech: no yeast is added, and wines are fermented on naturally occurring grape yeasts alone; and except for the vin de voile, they use no wood barrels. Their winegrowing is chemical free except for now state-mandated treatments against *cicadelles* (leafhoppers) that had spread vine-killing bacteria known as Flavescence dorée through southwest France, northern Italy, and Spain.

Before lunch, Bernard and I and a young customer who had driven from Lyon set about sampling the Plageoleses' range of whites in their tasting room. Through the open windows you could smell the end of the cool morning and the beginning of midday. We tasted many wines, but I was most interested in the Plageoles family legacy and ondenc. In its dry form it produced a wine that was soft in the mouth, a white reminiscent of chenin blanc in the Loire Valley.

As for the sweet wines made from ondenc, it took only a few sips to make me understand how profoundly it had transformed the Plageoleses into something more than winemakers.

Bernard explained the process for making the sweet ondenc wines: At the end of the growing season, four grape bunches are left on each vine, and instead of harvesting them, the Plageoleses simply pinch each bunch stem with pliers—severing the communication with the plant and allowing the grapes to dry and sweeten independently. Weeks later when the grapes are harvested, they are laid out in straw protected from rain in Plexiglas tunnels where they continue to dry and ripen, fanned by the region's hot Autan winds. Depending on the resulting sugar and alcohol level created that year, the wine is released as either a *vin moelleux* (semisweet wine) called "Caprice d'Autan" or as a higher-in-sugar *vin liquoreux* (sweet wine) labeled "Vin d'Autan."

Bernard poured glasses of the 2004 version labeled "Caprice." It smelled of figs and light spring flowers. Chilled in the mouth, it was lush nectar.

"Now I'm going to make you taste something," Bernard said. He led us outside and back to a hangar filled with steel, cement and fiberglass tanks of varying sizes, a hydraulic press, and bottling machines. He walked over to a fiberglass tank containing what could have been no more than a hundred gallons of liquid. In this case, the liquid was the 2005 version of sweet ondenc—a Vin d'Autan. The wine was at room temperature, a test that shames most sweet wines, turning them into cloying servings of syrup. But this wine was everything the first one was, only double—double the perfume, double the lush mouth feel, double the elegance.

I took a second sip and a third, making the spontaneous noises made by most mammals make when a virgin area of the brain's pleasure center is touched. And yet there was something disorienting about the whole scene. This Vin d'Autan was a wine of soaring quality, made all the more transcendent by the fact that it was sitting in a plain fiberglass tank in an open hangar in the countryside. How many experiences had I had like that? Some twenty years earlier, I remember pushing open a door to a small church by the side of the road in central Italy and finding, behind the old guardian who dozed on his broom handle, a collection of amazing Giotto-school frescoes. I had rarely experienced something so noble in such modest surroundings.

"You see," Bernard turned to me and said as if letting me on a secret that had defined the last quarter century of his life, "we are sort of the guardians of the temple here."

Later that afternoon, I had arranged to meet Plageoles, *père*. "I have to warn you, my father likes to talk," Bernard said. And when I returned I found Robert Plageoles, not merely talking but holding court to a pair of young couples—none of them more than twenty-five years old—who had driven up from Toulouse and were gazing at this short white-haired man in awe.

"Gaillac is one of the oldest *vignobles* of Gaul," Plageoles pronounced, looking at his audience over the metal rims of his eyeglasses. He stood in the winery in front of a row of old barrels used to raise his vin de voile. He wore a cotton vest, shirt, and jeans, and seemed to be thoroughly enjoying the role of professor emeritus. "No vignoble was chosen by hazard," he went on. "Particularly Gaillac. Intelligent men saw that Gaillac combined two climates—the humidity of the Bordelais with the heat of the Mediterranean."

"The *cepages* were perfectly adapted," he said, and then turned to me to ask for the English word for *cepage*. I explained that there was no word: that in English we spoke of "grape varieties."

"That's too bad," Plageoles said, frowning. Then he continued: "When a cepage has been used for five hundred years, it can be considered a cepage of Gaillac. Everything else is not a cepage of Gaillac."

Plageoles let that last thought sink in with his audience before launching into the first of many digressions of the afternoon—a mini-course on the Autan wind that brings the Mediterranean heat to Gaillac.

"Why is it called the *vent d'Autan*?" Plageoles surveyed the eager faces of his pupils. "One must never, never, never, never, never forget that we are in the land of Occitanie—and in the Langue d'Oc, *autan* means *autel* (church altar). It was called the *vent d'Autan* because it blew in the direction of the altars in the old village churches—from Jerusalem."

Completing the arc of his detour, Plageoles explained it is also these hot, drying winds, interspersed with periods of rain, that produces wine with the high alcohol and acidity content necessary to make vin de voile. In years when the conditions are not right, he doesn't bother.

"If you cheat nature, it will throw it back in your face something fierce," he said. "Nature, she is . . ." Plageoles crossed his hands in front of him as though he were running them over a piece of finely made marquetry. For a sound effect he clicked his tongue.

Plageoles had no formal education in wine, history, or linguistics. Rather, he was selected after his lycée studies to attend a prestigious preparatory school for engineers in Albi. His father, Marcel, however, had other plans for his only son.

"In the language of today," Plageoles said, "my father formatted me." Yet Plageoles was also shaped by his own raging curiosity, or as he put it: "I asked a lot of questions, and when you ask questions you have to answer them."

Plageoles then led us outside toward the ondenc vines planted by his father, stopping en route for another etymological detour as he explained the root of ondenc—named after a group of grape poachers from the village of Onde who were expelled for stealing the fruits of this early-maturing vine about five centuries ago.

He continued walking, and I asked Plageoles if there were not a central question that first set him on his path. He stopped in his tracks again. "I was born here. We Plageoleses have been here in Gaillac since the fifteenth century," he began. After a discourse on family genealogy, he continued: "I asked why is it that Gaillac, which had such a wine glory, somehow completely lost it?" How was it, Plageoles wondered, that the wines that were prized in England, Holland, and the north of Europe had fallen into near complete obscurity in the twentieth century?

As an inland wine producer, Gaillac faced difficulties and—for centuries—duties imposed by Bordeaux as it transported its wine by river to be shipped out of Bordeaux's Atlantic port. But the one factor that nearly killed Gaillac was "the quasi-mortal electroshock of phylloxera."

"Phylloxera didn't kill everything, but people reacted like they did for mad cow or avian flu. Everything was ripped up . . . everything." Following the outbreak, new, more productive varietals were introduced—grafted onto disease-resistant American rootstocks. To hear Plageoles tell it, in the late nineteenth century winemakers turned on their vines, and in a fit of hysteria held them responsible for the plague.

The forgetting vine.

We continued the last few feet to the patch of ondenc I had visited that morning with Bernard. Plageoles then explained how his father insisted on growing vines in large traditional open goblets, while most of his neighbors trained their vines on wires. Indeed, the goblet form was adapted to hot climates—as I'd learned from Didier

Barral. "Of course, we are in world of monkeys and parakeets, and everything now is adapted to the machines!"

But there was more to it than that. Plageoles bent down into a half squat. Each grape cluster, he noted, is protected by one leaf in particular—a leaf that acts as its "mother leaf." Only by letting the vines grow into their goblet form could vines grow as they were designed to grow, Plageoles said. Plageoles demonstrated the "mother leaf"—a concept he'd learned from a 200-year-old text—gently cradling a leaf in his hand. I looked around at the young men and women from Toulouse, who all seemed about ready to take this passionate and cantankerous old man in their arms and hug him.

The following morning I returned to chez Plageoles—this time to Robert Plageoles's house on the Domaine Roucou-Cantemerle in the adjacent village of Castelnau de Montmiral. Plageoles invited me here to this property overlooked by a farmhouse that he had bought in the 1960s to show me his two his most prized places.

I found Plageoles working in the vegetable patch next to the first prize, which Plageoles called his "conservatory." This conservatory was row after row of vines that he had grafted, cloned, and regrafted from the Domaine de Vassal at Sète—a state-run experimental estate and a sort of gene bank conservatory for thousands of species of wine and table grapes.

Plageoles directed my attention to two sections of vine rows planted about fifteen years earlier—perhaps three hundred plants in all. These rows contained two varietals: mauzac jaune and mauzac côte de melon (literally, yellow mauzac and melon-slice mauzac). Neither of these grapes, Plageoles said, had been used anytime recently for winemaking. "I am working here for the future," he said. His children's children.

Plageoles said he planted the vines and then watched them and tasted the grapes season after season. His conclusion thus far, he said, was that the mauzac côte de melon—so named because of the melonlike lines visible through the skin of the golden raisin—could make a great vin de voile. It has all the characteristics: high acidity, good maturity and sugar, and very little production. "It's a big question mark."

Then, as if he needed to explain why he had spent years cultivating grapes that might or might not make wine—and would probably not make wine that he would ever taste—Plageoles went on: "You know, I think that we human beings must plan. If human beings don't conserve and don't plan for the future, we don't really have a sense of existence. We are just born, grow old, and die with one goal in life . . . to make *fric* [cash]."

As we made our way to the neatly ordered house Plageoles shares with his wife, Josianne, I asked Plageoles about a statement that stretched across a brochure of Plageoles wines.

"Ce n'est pas le vin qui enivre. C'est L'homme que s'enivre."
—CONFUCIUS

[It's not wine that intoxicates. It's man who intoxicates himself.]

It seemed an audacious—certainly a politically incorrect—statement in an age when public sensitivities about the dangers of alcohol consumption seemed at their peak.

"We don't have a right to criticize wine," Plageoles said defiantly. "Modern society has classified wine as alcohol. Yes, it has alcohol in it along with many other things. But it is not alcohol!"

"Modernity simplifies everything—including our vocabulary," Plageoles said. Modern French, he noted, had one word for "field" whereas the Languedoc had thirty! "But, you know, I believe that that impoverishes us."

It was a cloudless spring morning and his extended family was arriving for the day—sons and daughters and a baby in a stroller. We went into the house and through a hallway on which hung Plageoles's small landscape paintings, then up a staircase through a pair of bedrooms and into a room filled with books from floor to ceiling. This was Plageoles's second prize—his library, with volumes on literature and philosophy, agriculture and wine, plants and insects, mushrooms and birds.

We stayed in that room about an hour, Plageoles showing me

old texts such as an original of Sebastian's *Traité pratique* with its reference to ondenc and Yquem. Then he brought down from a shelf the oldest book in his library—a red, leather-bound volume entitled *Cours complet d'agriculture* (Complete agricultural course), published by a French agricultural society in 1802. As Plageoles opened the book, he took obvious pleasure in touching the thick, soft white paper with its off-center blocks of text.

"It was here," Plageoles said, "that I found the concept of *la feuille mere* [the mother leaf]. Yes, of course, I understood before that plants in hot climates need shade, but the concept of the 'mother leaf' was . . . more poetic—it really *says* something. You know, I believe that the father of wine is the *vigneron*, and that the mother is the vine."

We sat in silence. I could hear that downstairs, in an open dining room sheltered from the sun, the table was being set for lunch. I thought of how different Gaillac and southwest France would be today if Plageoles had gone on to become an engineer. Perhaps he would have left a legacy of bridges or public buildings, or soccer stadiums. That would have been too bad for wine.

In traveling across the wine villages of France like Gaillac, I'd appreciated the lack of graffiti found almost everywhere else—on bridges, public buildings, soccer stadiums, or any blank wall or road sign. Logically, it may have something to do with the depopulation of the countryside: fewer youth to go astray. But I'd like to think it also has something to do with the vines connecting the generations with their history.

The mother leaf.

"You have to have that kind of rapport with vines you cultivate," Plageoles was saying. "You have to bring them closer to us—to humanity."

"If you don't . . . If you don't . . . " His voice trailed off. "If you don't . . . I think it's sad."

TEN

Heaven, Hell, or Burgundy

HARRY HAD A POINT.

I had known Harry and his wife, Joyce, for minutes: we were tablemates at the customary Diner de Gala aux Chandelles that follows the world's most famous wine auction at the Hospices de Beaune. As the main course arrived, Harry, who'd traveled all the way from Cleveland, Ohio, to savor these moments, explained to the others at our table (French, British, and one fellow American): "You could not have this meal in the United States!"

Surely nothing close to the setting exists in the New World. About six hundred of us were packed inside the great stone walls of a fifteenth-century fort covered with medieval tapestries and lit only by candles. But Harry wasn't talking architecture or history. He was talking about the nutritional divide between Europeans and Americans.

"In America," he went on, "the cholesterol police would be all over us." Of course, Harry was right. While Americans count "bad" grams, the French naturally seem to focus on their pleasure meter. (It's only in the last few years that the French government has tried to curb French excesses with anti-wine, anti-fat, anti-sugar, and anti-tobacco campaigns. But it was a tough sell, and the media were usually full of commentators who philosophized that all these efforts were "anti-pleasure.") The English language doesn't quite have a word that evokes the enjoyment of the sensual pleasures at the table as does the French verb *se régaler*. (The English offshoot "regale" doesn't muster the same uncomplicated hedonism.)

The main course, delivered with military precision by a battalion

11. My glasses, please: Candlelight dinner at the Beaune Hospices

of white-jacketed waiters, was a steaming ball of poached venison stuffed with foie gras and wild mushrooms. It was accompanied by the fourth wine of the evening—a red Burgundy from the cellars of the hospices.

"In fact," continued Harry, defiantly exuberant, "if my doctor— we'll call her Doctor X—could see us now, she would cast us into perdition!"

This Sunday night candlelight dinner is part of a long tradition involving charity and the fermented grapes that pay the bills. Over centuries the hospices have accumulated vineyards by donation, with the proceeds from the sale of wine going to pay for upkeep of the Hôtel Dieu—a fifteenth-century Flemish-style architectural masterpiece—and, since 1971, a modern hospital on the outskirts of town. Earlier that afternoon the hospices' wine, sold by the barrel, raised about five million dollars.

The dinner is also one of a trio of climaxes to what has become a weekend bacchanalia tied to the third Sunday in November, in which the population of Beaune—an otherwise orderly medieval town of about 23,000 inhabitants—doubles with hordes of costumed, parading, Burgundy-swilling revelers.

For the true aficionado, the Sunday candlelight dinner is the second of what are known as the *trois glorieuses*—a series of three glorious meals served around the auction. The first of the grand trio is Saturday night about ten miles north of Beaune and halfway to Dijon at Clos de Vougeot, where there's a meeting of the red-robed Confrérie des Chevaliers du Tastevin, the Burgundy-promoting order founded in 1934 with the motto *Jamais en vain, toujours en vin* (Never in vain, always in wine).

So here we were, my new friends from Cleveland and I, at what was my first glorieuse, and we had already been through pumpkin soup accompanied by a Pouilly-Fuissé 2000; the scallop ceviche with black truffles washed down by another Pouilly-Fuissé, a 2002; and the lobster ravioli accompanied by the last of the white wines, Corton-Charlemagne, a 2000.

We'd also been led by a folkloric musical group called Les Joyeaux Bourguignons, through half a dozen repetitions of the inevitable "Ban Bourguignon," the most popular of many Burgundian drinking anthems that seem to erupt spontaneously when any group larger than, say, two gets together to raise a glass.

It goes like this: *la-la la-la la-la ley-a* (while you hold your hands up next to your ears and twist them at the wrist from side to side). Then: *lalala lalala la-la lalalala* (while you clap on the beats). The second verse is the same thing but with a pronounced finale of *La! La! La!*

As Harry oohed and aahed over the venison and foie gras, these dozen merry minstrels—some who played instruments and others who cradled large glasses of red wine—led the crowd into another great drinking song: "Boire un petit coup" (Drink a little shot).

> *J'aime le jambon et la saucisse.* [Translation: Here the singer expresses his affection for ham and sausage.]
> *J'aime le jambon c'est bon!*
> *Mais j'aime encore mieux le lait de ma nourrice.* (But I like even better my nursemaid's milk.)

Just in case you haven't gotten the picture, these people like to party. Wine, food, and a fantastic capacity for their consumption—perhaps more so than in any part of France or the world—seem to be in the genes. The resistance movement to all those health campaigns finds a natural home here. It's also one of the rare places on earth that, even in the most luxurious trappings, manages to remain close to the earth.

Harry began to howl above the din. "What does my doctor—I mean Dr. X—know about having a good time?" Harry asked no one in particular. "NOTHING! If she were here she would be sitting in the corner eating a Saltine cracker . . . with no salt!"

It was not until 1 a.m. that the cheese course was brought out with a deep red 1995 Corton. About the same time a New Orleans–style jazz band came onto the small stage and brought down the house. Right there in the middle of this historic place, this bastion built by Louis XI, the crowd started drumming on the white linen–covered tables with dessert spoons and whatever other silver was left. As 2 a.m. approached, the band struck up "When the Saints Go Marching In," and it seemed the place would explode. Harry yelled something in my ear about France being a great country, and something else about Doctor X.

People were now not just drumming on the tables but drumming on bottles, coffee cups, and *each other*. After the band finished an encore and left the room, the drumming only became louder. A wine glass popped here, a coffee coaster there. A white-haired man old enough to be my grandfather stood on a chair with his fist raised in the air.

Luckily for those concerned, most people seemed to be making their way from the dinner on foot.

Had the weekend stopped there, I would have been content. One glorieuse would have been plenty. At a series of other lunches and dinners, I'd already eaten my way through countless courses including escargots in a crêpe-like envelope, frog ravioli swimming in basil and garlic, young rabbit wading in berries, and *epoisses* cheese with the odorous aura of an old coat.

I'd drunk my way through many a delightfully long and complex white Burgundy and many a soft, seductive red. And I'd swirled, chewed, gargled, and spat scores of other wines at tastings such as the sampling of the hospice's 2005 vintage in the hospice's "king's chamber" under a portrait of Louis XIV.

I'd even begun to *understand* Burgundy, which should be simple yet is anything but. It should be simple because Burgundy cultivates two principal grapes for fine dry wines—chardonnay for white and pinot noir for red—and most all wines are raised in oak barrels. But its classification system of eighty-seven appellations based on oddly named hyphenated villages (with their own dialectic pronunciations) and vineyards shared among some 3,500 winegrowers confuses most everyone, including most French.

Beaune sits at the edge of the middle of one of the world's most compact winegrowing regions, known as the Côte d'Or or "gold coast." This thirty-mile string of limestone-rich hillsides laced with ocean sediment runs southwest from Dijon through the section known as the Côte de Nuits, known for Burgundy's most sought-after reds, and then around Beaune turns into what is called Côte de Beaune, which produces Burgundy's most-prized whites around the Montrachet hillsides. Each village along the coast is divided into parcels that are often worked by scores of small producers, most of whom have winemaking operations in cellars excavated under their homes. Each parcel has its own qualities and pedigree based on altitude, soil, drainage, slope, and exposure that influence the taste of the wine. It's that terroir from one patch of land to the next that determines whether a pinot will conjure dark fruit, mushrooms, minerals, or something else as its aromas rise up from the glass. That terroir determines whether it will be brought to your table at a country café with a hearty dish of *œufs en meurette* (poached eggs in local pinot noir) or whether the wine will be out of reach for all but a few humans. The wines are simply all over the place. In most regions, a winemaker will offer you two or three wines of one color to taste from a given year, whereas in Burgundy he or she will pour out a dozen—each originating from a different subregion, village, or vineyard.

There are plenty of bad Burgundies. I've tasted my share of thin, bitter reds and schizophrenic whites at champagne prices. But I've also tasted straightforward, delicious Burgundies that cost less than breakfast in a Paris hotel—which explains why the addresses of small, reliable, and reasonably priced producers are kept preciously by Frenchmen who return year after year.

Very good Burgundies are among the most gorgeous wines I've experienced: at once elegant and strong, refined and earthy. The pleasures of a great Burgundy are often fleeting: they are music to the architecture of Bordeaux. Burgundy reds have been called "an iron hand in a velvet glove." They are wines that make you want to taste and taste again.

Most modern-style red wines pack a big upfront show of muscle—a fireworks display of fruit and tannin that explodes on the inside of the mouth and then disappears. Red Burgundy pinot noir—generally lighter, more ethereal than its New World counterparts—is known for its "length" or staying power. The notes of a good Burgundy slowly roll down the center of the tongue at least eight musical beats before they dissolve at the opening of the throat.

While all wines taste best as close to their area of production as possible, this is particularly true of Burgundy. It's one thing to make delicious wines that win contests. But to make particular delicious wines that combine with a particular cuisine to do a yin-yang dance on the palate, and then to have a whole lexicon of particular bawdy songs to consume them—*that*, to me, is terroir.

This pull of delightful excess was the reason my weekend in Beaune would not—could not—end on Sunday. And why I had to gird myself to survive one more day. For Monday was the day of the third of the trois glorieuses, the Paulée de Meursault at Château de Meursault, the world's greatest BYOB meal.

I'd lucked into an invitation to the Paulée, put on by the fine white wine producers of the village of Meursault, after making the acquaintance of Jean-Claude Bernard, director of his family's hotel Le Cep in Beaune. On Friday afternoon just after I arrived, Bernard mentioned that he had one extra place available at his table at the Paulée. I jumped at the opportunity.

Throughout the course of my weekend I began to understand exactly what sort of experience I was in for. Sunday evening, I was chatting in the lobby of Le Cep with Henry Bernis Alsobrook, a New Orleans lawyer, bon vivant, and Chevalier de Tastevin, who'd been collecting wines since his student days at Tulane after WWII.

"You ev-ah been to the Paul-ay?" Alsobrook asked in a Louisiana drawl.

No, I said.

Alsobrook's eyes sparkled and he snorted: "Henh."

He let the gravity of his reaction sink in, and about half a minute later said, "Well, it works like this—you sit down for lunch 'round noon and you get up 'round seven. And you drink ... all ... day ... long." At this point, Mrs. Alsobrook, who had arrived for dinner, rolled her eyes and half-clucked her disapproval at her husband's frank phrasing. I had the impression she'd been doing that for some decades.

Monday before noon, I met up with Jean-Claude's entourage at Le Cep. This included Jean-Claude's German friend Werner and Werner's French wife, as well as Jean-Claude's very young trophy wife from the Ukraine. It was a clear, cold day in Burgundy, and as Jean-Claude's Mercedes sedan headed south of Beaune, the car spoke to him in English, warning him to "slow down" when he was exceeding the speed limit and to "watch out" when in the presence of radar.

As we pulled up to the château, it seemed as if it were occupied by the entire local corps of the French gendarmerie. The place was swarming with blue uniforms and squared-off hats. They signaled us down a dirt path and into a parking place in the grass. Instinctively, my first thought was that these military men and women (the gendarmerie is part of the French army) were here to do what they usually do: guard the Republic by writing as many traffic tickets as possible. Surely at afternoon's end they would give an alcohol breath test to everyone with a pair of car keys in hand. And surely, if the Paulée lived up to its reputation, they could make their yearly quota in an hour or two.

"They're here just to watch the parking lot and make sure everything goes well," Jean-Claude assured me. He was deadpan. "They are *certainly not* here to make any trouble for us."

Jean-Claude pressed a button on his car key to pop open the trunk. Inside was a milk crate full of dusty wine bottles—about enough whites and reds for lunch with about twenty mortals outside of Burgundy. He and Werner shouldered the wine, and I was given a bucket full of ice.

As scores upon scores of us made our way to the château—well outnumbered by our bottles—I noticed that the gendarmes were nothing like their tough, humorless, slightly menacing stereotype. These gendarmes and gendarmettes were doing something I'd never seen gendarmes do: they were smiling. Judging by those smiles and the pleasantries they were exchanging with the invitees, it was evident there was some sort of understanding. But what sort? Christmas was a month away, and perhaps at the end of the day there would be some unopened bottles of Meursault in need of official removal.

Inside, in what had once been the winemaking halls of the old white stone château, eight hundred guests were packed elbow-to-elbow at long tables covered in linens. In front of each place setting were a row of glasses, a beautiful printed menu summarizing the afternoon's program, and a small pliable pamphlet on which we could note the wines we tasted that afternoon. The menu also contained an English translation of a quote by Salvador Dali: "He who knows how to taste doesn't drink wine any longer but tastes secrets."

I looked around the hall, and it seemed that, judging from the lineup of thousands of bottles set out, we would be sharing many secrets that afternoon. From the elegant reds of the Côtes de Nuits appellations of Chambolle-Musigny, Clos de Vougeot, and Vosne-Romanée to the world's most sought-after whites from the Montrachet hillside south of Meursault.

I diligently began by writing down the names of each wine at our table with the year and the producer on the allotted lines of the pamphlet. These written notes later proved important, as the rest of the afternoon is like a movie montage in my memory. By consulting my souvenir menu, I can recount the multiple courses: something called an ambrosia of lobster and green asparagus, followed by not one main dish but three—sea bass in sesame crust with onion confit and wild mushrooms, quail stuffed with foie gras and accompanied by a pastry of fresh grapes, and veal knuckle cooked seven hours in wine lees.

I do remember other things. Like the Joyeux Bourguignons once again taking the stage and the multiple recitals of "Bans Bourguignons" that became rowdier as the afternoon progressed. I remember bottles—at first white—being passed from table to table. I remember Jean-Claude, who sat two places down, signaling me to try a surprising Côtes de Beaune from Saint-Romain. "Did you taste it, Robert?"

In fact, I had half a dozen glasses before me and I had lost track of what was what. So I turned to the lady on my left, Bernadette Bergeret, an oenologist from a Burgundy family who now worked in Alsace, and I asked her, "Madame, would you mind sniffing this glass and telling me if this is the Saint-Romain?" Madame took the glass, sniffed, and shook her head no. I handed her another glass; she sniffed and smiled: "This is it." I had to rely on Madame's expert nose at least twice more that afternoon.

To my right, Werner in his prim jacket and tie said into my ear in accented German English: "If things continue like this, I am going to be gassed." His wife smiled from across the table. "*Ce soir* I will be cooked!" he shouted across to her, mixing his languages. Then, under his breath, he said to me, "It's a good thing I made love to her this morning!"

Part of the Paulée is an annual literary prize, and at one point this year's prize winner—novelist, essayist, and member of the French Academy Erik Orsenna—was introduced. Orsenna paid eloquent tribute to his fellow artists, these winemakers who worked with the soil to create something meaningful and far older than literature.

During Orsenna's poetic address, Werner leaned over and said into my ear, "I take it back. I am not going to be gassed. I am going to be *stoned*."

Orsenna's prize was a hundred bottles of Meursault.

As the afternoon went on, bottles were replaced by even bigger bottles—magnums and even larger jeroboams. My notes indicate that at 4 p.m. we switched from white wines to red wines. "Robert, you must try this Pommard!" someone said. I do remember a Vosne-Romanée having a lovely scent of fall and leaves, and how surprised I was that I could taste anything at all.

The Joyeux Bourguignons launched into a version of "La Bourguignon," an early-nineteenth-century anthem often called "La Marseillaise of Burgundy." The refrain goes like this:

Joyeux enfants de la Bourgogne
Je n'ai jamais eu de guigon
Quand je vois rougir ma trogne
Je suis fier d'être Bourguignon.
(Joyous children of Burgundy
I've never had bad luck
When I see my bloated face get red
I'm proud to be Burgundian.)

There was a cheese course and more red wines. Then two men in chef's whites and toques brought out a giant cake with sparklers. Someone reported back that two Japanese men had fled and in the parking lot were gasping, "O mon Dieu!" There were more "Bans Bourguignons" followed by a rendition of the old forlorn soldier's song to the elusive barmaid Madelon as hundreds of napkins twirled and swayed in the air.

I had long ago stopped writing on the pamphlet given to us, and just started making tick marks for every wine drunk that afternoon. At the end of the day, the thing was stained with red wine and I'd made forty-eight tick marks. When it was over, I looked at my watch: 7:30 p.m. I wanted nothing more than to do what everyone had counseled me you must do after a Paulée: fall into the sagging mattress that awaited me at my hotel on the outskirts of Beaune.

In the fresh night air of the parking lot, I noticed there were no more gendarmes—apparently their shift had ended before the Paulée had. Then Jean-Claude announced, "Maintenant on visite les caves." This was one part of the Paulée I wasn't up on. Five winemakers opened up their wineries for everyone to pass through and taste their new vintage in barrels using the little Tastevin cups that were given to us at the Paulée as souvenirs. We visited four of the five. In contrast to the grand château, they were typical (that is, small) properties with cellars and bottles covered in black mold as thick as attic insulation.

"What do you want to do now?" Jean-Claude asked our growing entourage in front of the last winery. A younger man with a toothy smile suggested something right out of one of those bawdy Burgundy drinking songs: that he would like to share Jean-Claude's wife's coat with Madame inside of it. Everyone had a laugh and we went back to the car.

"On a faim. On a soif!" Jean-Claude announced as we barreled through the countryside, his car chiding him to slow down.

Hungry? Thirsty? I asked Jean-Claude what he had in mind.

"Oh, just some sandwiches and maybe something to drink," Jean-Claude laughed.

In fact, what was in store for us was a late-night dinner in the town of Chagny at Lameloise, the beautiful three-star restaurant where a table set for about twenty-five people awaited us with another one of those lovely printed menus announcing another five-course meal. The evening was organized by a pair of brothers—Marc and Hervé Gantier—the former being the owner of the Caveau des Arches restaurant in Beaune, and the latter, a winemaker in the tiny village of Bizanet in the Corbières.

We gathered in the restaurant bar and at 10 p.m. Marc Gantier announced the restart of the gustatory debauch with, "On mange."

"Allez," said Hervé, the older and portlier of the brothers, "à boire."

I could now feel my face tingling and my cheeks burning, and en route to my seat I passed a mirror and noticed that my face had turned the color of pinot noir.

Hervé announced with a toothy grin that we would be participating in the *quatrième glorieuse*, a concept that seemed to be dangerously tempting fate. I am not overly superstitious, but were there not *three glorieuses* for a reason? If three represents the number of

Christian divinity, then perhaps four couldn't lead to anything but trouble. (The Four Horsemen of the Apocalypse?)

Four was also the number of hours during which we ate and drank our way through five courses that began with foie gras ravioli and concluded in the wee hours of Tuesday morning with a plate of desserts accompanied by a cloud of cotton candy served in a crystal glass.

At 2 a.m. Hervé was proposing another toast—champagne. I looked into his large, flushed face with its crimson, toothy smile and had the strange thought I might be staring at the devil. I had the feeling that without the help of "Dr. X" or anyone else, I'd stumbled on the entrance to perdition.

I awoke Tuesday morning after about four hours' sleep to a strange, foul smell in my hotel room—a smell like burned wool and singed flesh. As I moved about the room, I noticed the stench moved with me. That's because I was its source. I tried, and nearly succeeded in, washing the smell away with a long, hot shower.

That morning, I was to make one stop in the vines, driving up from Beaune northward and then west into the upper high Côtes de Nuits. My destination was the village of Chevannes, where a young winemaker, barely thirty, by the name of David Duband was getting known locally as a serious small producer of fine red wines.

To get to Chevannes, Duband had explained on the phone, I would need to climb through the hills of villages with tongue-twisting names—Magny-Lès-Villers, Villers-La-Faye, and Meuilly—and turn at a series of landmarks: a stop sign, a pharmacy. And when I arrived in Chevannes, his would be the last house on the right before the road disappeared into the vines and forests.

The morning was crisp and bright, and as I climbed those hills, I passed neatly ordered rows of small frozen vines, then high meadows and horse farms and stands of pine and oak and chestnut trees. There were no other cars on the road, and as I drove on toward Chevannes it seemed the closest I'd come to paradise in a long while.

The Moon, the Stars, and the Loire

So the angel swung his sickle on the earth and gathered the vintage of the earth, and threw it into the great wine press of the wrath of God; and the wine press was trodden outside the city, and blood flowed from the wine press, as high as a horse's bridle.
—REVELATION 14:19–20. The wine press scene is illustrated in the Tapestry of the Apocalypse (circa 1373) at Angers in the Loire Valley.

We are at a moment when the earth is rising up and revolting.
—NICOLAS JOLY, Coulée de Serrant, April 2006

IN THE FIRST DAYS OF SPRING 2006, the world as viewed from France seemed to be coming apart.

With the first sweet, warm breezes of the year came the smell of teargas in Paris. University and high school students—angry over what would prove to be short-lived labor reforms intended to create more jobs by making it easier for employers to hire and fire—blockaded campuses and took to the streets by the millions. It was a movement founded on a sort of only-in-France confused politics: where else did a nation's young go on strike before they had ever worked a day? It was a movement fueled by trade unions, hormones, coffee, cigarettes, and alcohol. At the fringes, storm-the-Bastille radicals and toughs from the suburbs used the moment to serve up the cliché of their discontent: made-for-television images of *automobiles flambées*.

12. Nicolas Joly and the Coulée

Meanwhile, in the vineyards, as the first buds popped from the vines, one of the covenants of French winemaking quietly died. In late March the French agricultural ministry approved the use of wood shavings in wine—something hitherto regarded as heresy.

The principals of wood and wine are simple. Different varieties of wine are raised in wood barrels before bottling, traditionally as a way to allow for a slow oxidizing effect and to impart tannins that complement those in the wine. Among fine winemakers, wood shavings are regarded as an industrial shortcut or cheat—"oaky" flavoring additive that hides the true character of the wine. Makers of French wine-by-the-tanker had argued that banning wood chips was an anachronism that was inhibiting France's ability to compete with the New World, Australia, and South Africa.

In French journals a few purists were quoted crying "scandale," but they were drowned out by more pressing cries du jour. Among the "scandale" warning camp was Nicolas Joly, the nature healer of France's vineyards, a leader of the anti-chemical crusaders, and the godfather of biodynamic winemaking the world over. In the Loire Valley outside the village of Savennières, he is also the maker of one the most exquisite white wines anywhere. To Joly, I would learn, the student protests, the violence, and the wood chips were related on some profound cosmic level: all examples of flaws in human consciousness in a world that was living out of balance.

Biodynamic agriculture was the brainchild of Rudolf Steiner (1861–1925), the Austrian philosopher, educator, literary scholar, and spiritualist who in the last years of his life advocated a new form of holistic farming that went well beyond organic—seeking to align the work of the land with forces of nature, the moon, and the stars.

It was pretty heady stuff. And in recent years it's become trendy as well. At every wine fair and through every trip through the vine-yards, I met more and more winemakers who announced they were in the process of going *biodynamique*. Joly's book *Wine from Sky to Earth: Growing and Appreciating Biodynamic Wine*, first published in 1999, has now been printed in nine languages. In Alsace, a region not known for frivolity, serious winemaking families were burying cow horns full of crystals or cow dung to make special soil and plant preparations. Small young vintners were returning to the use of plow horses. And big names such as the Rhône winemaker-broker Chapoutier and Burgundy's elite Domaine Romanée Conti had embraced biodynamics as a way of returning life to their vineyards. The arc of Joly's influence extended from his fellow local winemakers in Savennières and the Loire to almost every winegrowing region of the world including California, where the Benziger Family Winery of Sonoma touted biodynamics as a means of bringing the French concept of terroir to their eighty-five-acre estate.

Most of it seemed to make good practical sense. After all, farmers have been working with natural remedies and astronomy for mil-lennia. But the practices of some adherents seemed questionable to me. For example, on one trip to Burgundy, I was more than skepti-cal when a young winemaking couple insisted that before tasting wine at around 9 a.m., we consult the lunar calendar to see how the wine would be affected at this particular hour of the day. I told them that I found wines to vary more based on the coffee clock: how many hours (or in this case minutes) after breakfast they were consumed.

I traveled most of the way across France to meet Joly, arriving in his world on a morning when a general strike crippled the country and France needed some healing.

Joly presides over what is known as the Coulée de Serrant. After driving up a long dirt road outside Savennières, I found myself overlooking the *coulée* (small valley) and the most majestic estate I'd seen in France—impressive even by the Loire Valley's regal standards. The coulée opens up to a panorama of the Loire. On either side of the coulée, enclosed by medieval walls and gates, are slopes covered with the dominant grape of Savennières—chenin blanc, which produces fragrant, honey-colored white wines that vary (depending on vintage and vineyard) from dry to semisweet. About seventeen acres comprise the Savennières–Coulée de Serrant appellation, one of a few exclusive-to-one-estate appellations in France that had once impressed French kings from Louis XI to Louis XIV.

Tucked into the deepest side of the valley is the Joly home— the twelfth-century monastery built by Cistercian monks who also planted the first vineyards here. Around back are the stables for Joly's farm animals, including a breed of Nantaise cattle that provides the vineyard fertilizer; a white-speckled work horse that pulls the hand plow in the oldest vine rows, which are too narrow for a tractor; and a small herd of short-legged Brittany sheep used for keeping cover crop trimmed between vine rows.

The entry road continues on a plateau above the western slope of the coulée to the winery in an eighteenth-century manor. Alongside this dirt road, on a cliff perched above the Loire, is an alley of ancient cypress tress sheltering a few moss-covered stone tombs of English soldiers who died here in the famous battle of Roche-aux-Moines, nearly eight hundred years ago.

I was greeted by Joly's daughter, twenty-seven-year-old Virginie, a sincere young woman with long, straight brown hair, wearing blue jeans and no makeup. The eldest of the Jolys' two children, Virginie had embraced her father's agricultural methods and joined him in overseeing the family vineyards along with four full-time laborers. She led me through a hallway filled with hunting trophies to a library with lived-in velvet chairs and books stacked helter-skelter on shelves that climbed to the ceiling. Large windows overlooking the vineyards and the Loire were framed with drapes of antique blue monochrome Toile de Jouy. Virginie left and a woman in a maid's tunic entered and asked me what I might like to drink. It wasn't the kind of place I'd expected—far too aristocratic and not quite granola-feeling.

As Joly entered the room, he seemed to fill it. He was the picture of a gentleman farmer: tall with a high forehead, graying temples, and wire-rimmed glasses, he wore corduroy pants and a weathered leather hunting vest. The only outward symbol of his nature-healer philosophy was a pair of leather Birkenstock sandals.

He handed me a business card, insisting that I read it. Under his name, printed in classical flowing script, was printed in English his sine qua non: "Nature assistant and not wine maker."

As we settled into the plush chairs, the maid brought me a glass of sparkling water. Joly warned me that what I was about to drink was very high in mineral content. He took the bottle off the maid's service tray and started reading the fine print on the label. "The body retains the minerals," he said. "It's bad for the joints—if you drink this all the time you'll be all mineral." The woman left the room and returned minutes later to bring Joly a pot of tea.

Joly grew up hunting and fishing in the Anjou, this region of the Loire Valley surrounding the small, prosperous city of Angers. His father was a surgeon who bought Coulée de Serrant in the 1960s and Joly's mother managed the vineyards. About that same time, when many of his peers were rejecting capitalism, Joly embraced it—traveling to New York to get his MBA from Columbia University. He worked for several years as an investment banker for Morgan Guaranty in New York and later London. "I was in an idealistic period," Joly laughed, and then he spoke the only sentence of English of the day: "I said, let's make money!"

After a few years as a highflying financier, Joly began questioning his career. His bank director in London, Joly remembered, complained to a group of young bankers including Joly, "I am a slave to luxury."

"When he said that, something clicked," Joly recalled. It proved a turning point in his life. His father had recently died and his mother needed help back at the estate. "Back then, wine made no money. But I said, 'I will go back. I will make minimum wage for a while, but I will be free.'"

Of course, going back to the coulée was not going go back to an ordinary patch of dirt. Maurice Edmond Sailland (1872–1956), who used the pen name "Curnonsky" and was known as the prince of French gastronomy, had classified Coulée de Serrant in the company of Yquem and Montrachet as one of France's great white wines. "It was run *à l'ancienne*," Joly said. Under his mother's management, few chemicals or fertilizers were used. Convinced that his legacy lay in modernizing the estate, Joly hired consultants and explored the latest farm technologies.

"I was a modern manager—I brought in herbicides, chemical fertilizer, and insecticides. . . . And then after two years I went into the vineyard and I saw that I had destroyed something. The color of the soil had completely changed. It became paler, and harder. The insects, the ladybugs, were no longer here."

Joly said that up to this point in his life he'd had little regard for ecologists. "To me ecologists were city people who knew nothing about nature." Then in 1979 a friend in Paris passed along a book to him about Steiner and biodynamic agriculture, and again his life took a turn.

Biodynamics hadn't yet been applied to winemaking, and Joly decided to experiment with it on one hectare (almost two and a half acres). "The challenge was, how would I explain this to the workers of the estate?" he said. He cut out the chemicals, had the workers turn the soil with horse and plow, used organic soil preparations, and applied healing herbs to the plants and soil—all timed to the celestial calendar.

Joly himself was afraid. But in the first year, the small plot that Joly dedicated to biodynamics was the first in the vineyard in which the grapes reached full maturity. By 1984 the whole vineyard was working on biodynamic principles. With the passion of a reformed sinner who's been born again, over the next hour Joly described his gospel of the laws of nature, condemning the follies of modern agriculture.

He started by talking about the twin polarities of the earth and sun—gravity and light—each force contributing to a continuous circle of expansion and contraction. "Now we are passing into spring. And what is spring?" Joly suddenly lifted himself out of his chair and stretched his arms upward. "The days are longer than night, which means that the force from the air is stronger than the earth."

"This liberates the vine from gravity . . . ," Joly said as he opened his arms and looked up toward the ceiling, miming a flower straining up toward the sky. "Sickness in plants occurs when there is something missing in the link between earth and sky." Joly sat back down and crossed his legs.

"Goethe said if you want to understand the microcosm you have to understand the macrocosm. When you look at a soil in a microscope, it's like a guy from an undeveloped country who sees people on a television screen and then tries looking inside the television for the people. . . . That's the kind of error we made in agriculture."

Joly then launched into a recitation of what he calls the *quatres drames* (four tragedies) of modern farming. "The first tragedy—herbicides," Joly said, explaining how, in the postwar years and the flight from the countryside, herbicides presented what seemed a practical and non-labor-intensive way to take the place of working the soil. "But no plant can live without microorganisms in the soil, and the herbicides killed all the microorganisms. So to make up for the lack of the food in the soil, we added chemical fertilizers—the second tragedy."

Joly stood, rummaged around on an antique table, and produced a photograph of a vine from Beaujolais—unearthed with its roots intact. The main root of the vine extended downward several yards and then at one point turned upward in a 45-degree angle. This,

Joly said, was the moment in the plant's life when chemical fertilizers were introduced. Rather than searching deeper for its nutrients (an exploratory process that eventually imparts complex flavors to wine), the root stalk had turned upward to eat the elements at the surface.

What's more, Joly said, back in his chair, chemical fertilizers are high in salt content, forcing the vines to take more water. More water, he said, meant more problems with mildew. "We forced the vines to drink too much and that is why all the vines of France suffer from rot!"

And that was only the half of it. There were still, by my calculation, two tragedies to go.

To correct the chemical imbalance created by overfertilizing, Joly went on, the third tragedy was born: the systemic treatments that penetrate into the plant sap. "And what is sap?" Joly asked, barely pausing to breathe. "Sap is the plant's telephone for talking to the sun. If you poison the sap, you cut off the plant's ability to communicate with the sun and you poison the plant's capacity to control the taste, smell, and color of fruit."

Joly pulled a handkerchief out of his vest pocket and sneezed into it. He took a sip of his tea. His golden retriever, La Lune, entered the room, planted herself in front of me, and insisted on giving me her paw over and over. "Modern agriculture," he said softly, "guarantees a big harvest but destroys all the original taste of the fruit."

With each tragedy, each ecological scandale, Joly's sap was rising. It was not difficult to see where his argument was going. To make great wine you need great fruit. Industrially produced grapes were the equivalent of supermarket strawberries—a shadow of the real thing. And sitting here in his study—with the Loire and one of France's most beautiful vineyards visible through the glass terrace door behind him—the point seemed all the more profound.

One more tragedy to go. One more tragedy to push Joly's own sap to its apogee. The fourth tragedy, was after all, the tragedy of unforgivable tragedies, the one-way street to the innermost ring of the inferno.

"Technology," Joly said.

"Technology?" I asked, disappointed. I had been expecting something more nefarious and less friendly. Something more *dramatique*.

Because winemakers were left with tasteless fruit, Joly explained, modern winemaking had to come up with technological tricks to restore some "characteristic flavors." And in Joly's conception, the most heinous of the unforgivable tragedies is the fermenting of wine with flavor-enhancing yeasts.

While chenin blanc and most other wine grapes require no added yeasts to begin fermentation (Joly uses none), most winemakers the world over do add some yeast. The most traditional winemakers either use none or opt for "neutral" selected yeasts derived from the grapes themselves. But winery suppliers proudly advertise hundreds of yeast varieties that "bring out" aromas in wine, from plum to berry to earth and spice in reds, to clove, pear, melon, almonds, and even pineapple in whites.

"It is *scandaleux*," Joly proclaimed, narrowing his case down to the example of the Beaujolais Nouveau produced by that region's biggest winemaker and reseller, Georges Duboeuf. In the making and marketing of Beaujolais Nouveau—a cheap young red in a region that actually does produce some quality wine from gamay grapes—Duboeuf used a house yeast that gave off a distinctive banana smell. In recent years after complaints about the "Chiquita effect," Duboeuf changed to a yeast that produced more of a dark fruit effect.

"For twenty years he used the banana yeast. And because of that the Japanese are convinced that Beaujolais has the taste of banana!" Joly said. "Now it's been three years they replaced the banana with cassis. And somewhere in Paris a sommelier says, 'Ahhh! What a taste of cassis in the Beaujolais!'"

"It is *ab-so-lu-ment scan-da-leux*!"

It was about all the scandal and tragedy I could take in one day, and at this point I suggested we leave the office to have a look at the vines. We hopped in Joly's Jeep, which he drove across the coulée

The Moon, the Stars, and the Loire 169

and up to the far end. "For me, agriculture is music and biodynamics is acoustics," he said.

Indeed, the coulée looks like a great amphitheater facing the Loire. It has the natural elements needed for making a great wine: southern-exposed slopes, a poor subsoil of schist laced with quartz, and a microclimate that cools off the vineyard on summer evenings and encourages a hint of botrytis or "noble rot," the same beneficial fungus that flourishes in the Bordeaux Sauternes to produce some of the world's most profoundly fragrant sweet white wine.

We walked through the vines to the edge of the vineyard enclosed by a wall made from layers of stacked schist. At the top of the ridge was an iron gate, which Joly opened, revealing another vineyard that sloped down to small patches of forest and the Loire. This vineyard, just outside the sheltered contours of the coulée, produces Joly's basic Savennières wine.

All Joly's vineyards are cultivated with the same biodynamic principles. The care he gave to his vines resembles more the rejuvenating treatments at an expensive spa than any common conception of agriculture. Beginning in spring, Joly sprays his earth and vines with teas. He mists his vines with a seaweed tea—a protection from burning in the hot sun—which is essential, Joly said, because of the degradation of the Earth's ozone layer. He also sprays teas of garlic, which he said "revive the old vines and makes them young." The third tea that he systematically sprays over his vineyard is from nettle. To describe the beneficial effects of this wildflower (commonly drunk as a tea—used by Europeans as a spring purifying tonic), Joly closed his eyes and moved his hands in a circular motion: "Nettle is a plant that helps the circulation." Horsetail, a rich source of silica cherished by the Romans (who ate it raw) as well as American Indians (who used it to treat flesh wounds) is sprayed on the soil. Oidium, the powdery mildew that attacks vines after periods of rain, is one of the chief nuisances to wine producers. Organic growers usually fight it by spraying sulfur on the vines after each rain. Less attentive winemakers periodically break out the chemical fungicides. What does Joly do for his vines? He sprays dilutions of cow's milk (organic from a neighbor) in the vineyard during susceptible periods—when, he said, the moon is closest to the earth and the weather is damp.

But the Joly method is not all about picking wildflowers for his plant concoctions. Sometimes nature must be fought with fire. Long ago, Joly found that righting his vineyard with the forces of nature didn't stop the local rabbit population from hopping around his vines, eating the new growth and reproducing. "There are," Joly said in a matter-of-fact way that would surely alarm some animal rights activists and vegetarians, "the incinerations."

The incinerations are Joly's preferred method of biodynamic pest control. The recipe is as follows:

— Capture one animal of the offending species.
— Slaughter and skin.
— Thoroughly incinerate skin in a hot fire.
— Collect incinerated skin. Slice, dice, and grind to a powder in mortar.
— Spread said pelt powder over vineyard (a couple of spoon-fuls per acre will do) when the planets are aligned such that Venus is in Scorpio (mid November through early December).
— Repeat every season for four years.

It is practices like this that lead some to suspect biodynamics of being a sorcerer's cult. (Eye of newt, anyone?) But there are often reasonable explanations behind it. Take, for example, Joly's bunny burning. "All animals guide themselves by smell," Joly explained. By spreading the ashes of their pelts around in the period of high fertility, the animals can detect what's good for them and hightail it out of there. "You discourage animals from reproducing *chez vous*." Joly insisted that the same method works for other species—burning whole garden snails and grasshoppers, for example, to keep those pests away (though the period for burning is in spring).

Just before lunch, we returned to the farm manor and entered Joly's winery, housed in the cellar. This was also not what I expected: it was a rustic, cramped, low-tech affair with a hydraulic press and a few steel fermenting tanks of different sizes. There were no computers, no control panels that monitored what was going on inside the tanks. There was, in fact, *nothing* much at all. Joly's cellar master doesn't even try to control the temperature of fermentation. "When your agriculture is good," Joly said, "your cellar becomes a maternity ward, not a factory."

Joly led me into a cellar room where 500-liter barrels containing his 2005 vintage were reposing. (Joly lays his wine down in these oversized oak barrels for about nine months. He rotates out the barrels about every nine years.) Sticking with his maternity analogy, Joly explained why the "scandale" of using wood chips was an illusion. Joly believes—and *this I must warn is a point where things get esoteric*—that the shape of the barrel in the life-giving form of an egg is also important in birthing the new wine. Joly then described his interest in keeping wine in clay amphorae, which the Romans used to store wine for centuries. "Look at the shape of an amphora—it's an antenna that points straight down to earth!" Joly exclaims. "Wine is Dionysus and Dionysus is the earth. The antenna is pointing straight down to Dionysus!"

I asked Joly if he'd tried using amphorae instead of barrels. "Yes, last year," he said, "but the amphora wasn't waterproof and the wine all leaked out." The thought of Coulée de Serrant leaking on a basement floor was tragic, even if it was going in the direction of Dionysus. Amphorae, Dionysus, and ash of hare! All of it might be dismissed except for the fact that Joly makes beautiful wines beyond reproach.

We climbed a set of stairs to the main floor and returned to Joly's study, where he brought a pair of glasses and three bottles containing the 2004 vintage of each of his wines. Tasting Savennières wines is always a treat because of the surprise involved. The wines—which can be dry, off-dry, or semisweet—vary from vintage to vintage and from vineyard to vineyard based chiefly on the maturity of the fruit and its degree of noble rot. The wines also have nothing in common with wines from anywhere else: there's none of the crisp, citrus bite found in sauvignon blanc or pinot gris, nor any of the buttery vanilla of a big chardonnay.

We started with Joly's basic Savennières, called Les Vieux Clos.

The color was glistening honey. It tasted of flint robed in an aromatic, ever-so-slight hint of sweetness. Another thing, it was served at room temperature. Joly's winery has no refrigerator, as he believes refrigeration masks a wine's true character—and defects. Joly also says his wines resist oxidation and often get better a full day after they are opened.

Next we moved onto Joly's middle wine—harvested in a sub-appellation called Savennières–Rôche aux Moines, which Joly shares with three other producers. This wine, called Clos de la Bergerie, was everything the first was—only more so.

Then came the Coulée de Serrant, ever darker, limpid, and smelling of the first flowers of spring. It was like nothing I'd even imagined from a wine. It danced across the tongue so lightly and then seemed to waft up through my sinuses before it slowly dissipated in the upper brain lobes. There was nothing Dionysian about it. The stuff was pure liquid velvet.

Joly then rummaged through a pile on the table and unearthed a series of black-and-white photographs resembling Tibetan mandalas. These were photographs taken of crystallizations, the method developed by Steiner for graphically representing the life patterns in liquids. Crystallizations are done by adding copper chloride to a liquid and letting it dry in a petri dish. The crystal pattern when dry resembles the ice crystal pattern you find on your car windshield in the morning after a hard freeze.

He showed me a sample of human milk and another pattern showing powdered processed milk, then a crystallization using organic potato before and after irradiation. The original "real" products produced perfectly symmetrical patterns of thousands of fibers that radiated out from a common center. The "altered" products were changed in some way: they have multiple nucleuses or have lost their center.

Then Joly produced a crystallization of Coulée de Serrant—showing all its life force through a symmetrical web—and a sample of the same wine after being run through a supermarket scanner. "You see," he said, "Just something like that . . . it breaks the wine. It reduces its force."

In the Jeep on the way to his home for lunch, Joly spoke about increased earthquake activity, climatic change, man's tampering with electrical fields in the atmosphere, and the huge debts owed by industrialized nations. "We are at a moment when the earth is rising up and revolting," Joly said. His view for the future is nearly apocalyptic.

"I fear that the world is heading for a big crisis. And wine, wine is a luxury product. I tell my children, 'We are living in the last great years of wine.' As for me, with my cows I am autonomous. . . . Of course, the only thing on which I depend from the outside world is gasoline and airplanes."

Before turning into the entrance of the monastery, we passed a birch tree with a plastic water bottle attached to its side. A plastic tube inserted into the bark dripped a pale whitish liquid into the bottle. I asked Joly if the tapping of the birch sap is another medicinal recipe for his vines. "Oh, no, it's for me," he said. "I drink it." Unlike mineral water, birch sap is apparently good for the joints.

We ate lunch with Virginie at the large round wood table in Joly's rustic dining room. Lunch was deviled eggs from Joly's chickens, couscous and carrots from his vegetable plot, stewed apples from his trees, and a bottle of Coulée de Serrant that Virginie poured into a carafe and swirled vigorously.

Over lunch, the conversation went in all directions. Joly discussed the political crisis that faced France, globalization, the cowardice of the wine press, the effect of cellular telephone frequencies on the environment, and wine. I had the impression that he could have a dozen conversations at once and not lose track of any of them.

Joly looked at the world glut of wine and concluded that there were two ways for France to deal with it. One way was for France to chase short-term consumer tastes. Hence the wood chips. "But that will last two or three years. In the long term it is not by trying to appeal to consumer tastes that one is going out of the crisis. . . . The consumer will realize that all technological wines taste the same."

Here for a moment I caught a glimpse of a different Joly. Instead of Joly the biodynamic advocate, it was Joly the banker speaking. He explained in balance-sheet terms why French wines cannot compete in the world of cheaper wines. "It takes ten years for a winery to return capital investment in France," he said. "In Chile, it takes three."

To Joly there was but one way for France to rise out of the crisis and remain a world leader in wine, and that was "for France to sell the richness of France." France must continue to "up" the level of wine quality: France and Italy, he said, have some of Europe's and the world's greatest diversity of geology and microclimates, which makes them ideal for making great terroir wines. "*Terroir* is like a musical instrument," he said. "And France is overloaded with beautiful instruments."

"We lack for one thing," he sighed. "We just lack the musicians."

On my way back home by high-speed train, as the French countryside passed in a blur, I read from Joly's book—a mix of theory, practical advice, recipes for winemakers, and metaphysics.

My encounter with Joly had left an impression that would make it hard for me not to look at the world in a different light. Once I was home, that impression would lead me to seek out certain wild plants to use in teas in my garden and on the few dozen vines I'd recently planted there. Doing that would not be easy. When I asked the manager of the local agriculture cooperative about getting my hands on horsetail—*prêle* in French—he chortled as if choking on an escargot. "Most people who ask me about it want to find a way to get rid of it," he said after recovering.

Horsetail may be one of the world's most ancient plants—dinosaurs having snacked on huge ancient varieties—and its odd bulbous flowers may be a spring delicacy in Japan. But in most of the modern Western world, it is considered an invasive weed. He said he was sure some of his customers would be glad to pass their horsetail infestations on to me. He wished me good luck in finding some, told me to look along stream banks, and just for good measure added: "In my opinion, you'll be back in a couple of years for some herbicide."

We did find horsetail. I bought some dried leaves at an herbalist/

pharmacy for making tea (apparently good for middle-aged joints and muscles). And my wife discovered a patch growing wild by a tree along a riverbed. She dug up some of this nuisance plant and we planted it in our garden in a confined bed framed by stone walls. After months of nursing the plants, they died.

The souvenirs of my trip to Coulée de Serrant are now resting in the Dionysian part of the house—my wine cellar. Still, I've wondered if the coulée is the definitive laboratory for biodynamic winemaking. After all, long before Joly took over, the vineyard was already producing something close to miracles. In other words, this was no ordinary patch of land. Its particular position between earth and sky has long produced heavenly results. I doubt that, in the years to come, when my grapes are ready for harvest, the results will be quite the same. My patch of hillside is an area long known for producing a bitter wine from a grape called *framboise*, which according to local legend had the characteristic of making people insane.

The coulée, to paraphrase Joly, was already a Stradivarius. Still, Joly has accomplished a not-so-easy feat: proving himself a musician worthy of his instrument.

Where Goes Chatus

AFTER LEAVING NICOLAS JOLY in the Loire, my senses were attuned to circumstances, events in everyday life, the phases of the moon, the cosmic ecology, and discreetly hidden meanings. Then chatus came along.

If the world were directed by intangible forces—wavelengths, light, vibrations, planetary forces, and even ideas, as Joly proselytized—could it be that I stumbled, by mere coincidence alone, on a wine of such unusual character, yet virtually unknown outside of a small corner of France?

I'll explain.

My wife went to Nice with a friend one day in the winter of 2006 and ate lunch in a local wine bar—actually a wine shop with four lunch tables and a *plat-du-jour*. The place proposed as its red-du-jour, that day, a vin de pays from the southern Ardèche called chatus.

The Ardèche is France on the wild side: a rugged, rural French administrative department straddling the frontiers of Mediterranean France and the cooler gray climes of the country's heartland, so sparsely populated that the average school has fifteen children. The southern Ardèche is the last gasp of Provence—the limit for olive trees and the garrigue of wild thyme and rosemary and lavender. It's a countryside of limestone canyons and the rounded profile of the Cevennes Mountains, of rivers favored by kayak and canoeing enthusiasts, and of a certain vibe that attracts old hippies.

The upper part of the Ardèche follows the Rhône up to some distinguished northern Rhône wine villages such as Cornas, Con-

13. Christophe Reynouard sampling chatus

drieu, and Saint-Joseph. There are no prized wine appellations in
the southern Ardèche. Among French law enforcement, the area is
distinguished for another area of agricultural exploitation: mari-
juana.

My wife brought me home a bottle of chatus, which we opened
that evening. It was a 2003 vintage called Monnaie d'Or, or "gold
coin." (I would later learn that the Latin root of the word *chatus*
referred to a small gold piece.) This vin de pays was produced by

the La Cévenole wine cooperative in Rosières; its label noted that the wine received a gold medal at the Paris agricultural salon. I was expecting a nice "little" drinkable wine. What I found instead was a glass of pure surprise.

The wine was a deep purple, and when I sniffed it there was an explosive bouquet of . . . what exactly is hard to say, but the words that kept popping into my head were "tanned," "fruit," "leather." In my mouth I sensed a big tannic wallop, which was followed by a long flavorful ride with a pleasant acidity. There were hints of the Medoc, of the Rhône Valley, of Burgundy's Côte de Nuits. The wine had power, it had finesse, but it was, at the same time, simple. If it were music, it would not be a Burgundian symphony, but one sustained electric chord played on the center of the tongue.

Just after Easter, we followed that chord through the Ardèche to investigate.

The La Cévenole wine cooperative sits on the southeast side of route D104, a two-lane road that cuts through the center of the sleepy agricultural town of Rosières. It is a typical block of a utilitarian building—built just before World War II—that serves as the economic center of a community of growers who for the last several generations have brought their grapes here.

When the cooperative was built, it was intended to empower local grape growers who had been at the mercy of resellers offering rock-bottom prices for wine grapes. In 1940, the first year that the cooperative turned out its own wine, grape prices to growers tripled.

Cévenole is a reference to the Cevennes Mountains, the first hills of which begin just a few yards behind the D104 on the opposite side of the street as the cooperative. The area has long cultivated a surprising diversity of grapes: mostly viognier for white wines and a mix ranging from gamay to cabernet and syrah for reds. And there is chatus.

I arranged to meet Frederic Allamel, the cooperative's cellar master, in the early morning and was greeted by a tall, studious-looking man with glasses, barely forty years old, who could pass for a history professor were it not for the stains of purple penetrating deep into the lines of his hands.

Allamel hails from a long line of winegrowers; his grandfather was one of the co-op's founders. Traditionally, Allamel explained, all grapes grown were mixed, fermented, and eventually bottled together indiscriminately—separated only by color for red or white wine. "The old grandpas always used to say, 'If you want to make a good wine, put chatus in the *cuve* [vat],'" Allamel said.

Chatus, Allamel pointed out, is one of France's oldest grape varieties and one of only several dozen listed by Olivier de Serres, considered the father of French agriculture, in his *Théâtre d'agriculture* (1600). Chatus's home is the Ardèche, but it also grows in an area of the Italian Piedmont around Cuneo under the name *nebbiolo di dronero*. There, as in the Ardèche, it also has been traditionally mixed with other varietals to provide body and structure to local wines.

From the 1950s to the 1980s, chatus all but disappeared from the Ardèche—principally because of the difficulty of cultivation. One challenge, Allamel explained, was that the hearty old chatus vines, planted on antique American rootstock known as Jacquez (or black Spanish), required a particular pruning technique. Whereas most vines are cut back to the second bud of the shoot, the old chatus vines planted here require winegrowers to cut back to the fourth bud. Vines incorrectly cut bore no fruit because the first three buds produce virgin shoots. Another problem was the narrow window of harvest, which was considered far too finicky. "Two days before its peak, chatus loses all its aromas. Two days later it is too late," Allamel said. "It is like a peach—it is best just before it rots."

In other words, chatus hardly seemed worth it. Most growers found it easier to pull up their vines and replant with modern, more-productive cloned varietals. By 1988 there were only about five acres of old chatus vineyard left intact. Most of it belonged to Allamel's family vineyards, run by his father, where one chatus plot of vines dates to 1883.

For the cooperative's fiftieth anniversary, the Cévenole winemakers decided to experiment with the old chatus from the Allamels' vineyard. For once, the chatus would be isolated and not mixed in with other grapes. The first test used a fermentation technique of carbonic maceration—a method commonly used in Beaujolais to produce light, fruity wines. But even using this technique, the wine turned out large, aromatic, and loaded with tannins, leading the Cévonole's winemakers to believe they were onto something.

The co-op and local growers started a replanting program, filling about a hundred acres with chatus. They quickly realized that the plant favored the slopes of the Cévonole with its sandy granitic soils over the limestone on the other side of the D104. They also observed that chatus seemed to take best near the areas and elevations where there were stands of chestnut trees.

The cooperative practices a reasoned agriculture—banning most uses of herbicides and systematic chemical treatments among its growers. The cooperative began making chatus in the late 1990s— now producing about 25,000 bottles. After a long fermentation, the wine is allowed to run off without pressing and then laid down for a year in Burgundy barrels before passing another year in cement tanks prior to being bottled and sold in the co-op shop for the grand sum of 6.70 euros. The entire production is released in December and sells out by March—almost entirely to Ardèche locals—long before the summer tourists arrive. Only a few dozen bottles, such as the one my wife purchased in Nice, ever manages to slip out of the Ardèche.

As Allamel and I were speaking in front of the cooperative, Hervé Thoulouze pulled up in his tiny Renault Clio. A man who is built like a cement piling with a shaved head and a neck that resembles a cinderblock, Thoulouze had to squeeze out of his toy car. If it weren't for the small earring hoop in his left ear, and the light tan moustache floating in a couple days of stubble, you could mistake him for an army drill sergeant. He wore a military green T-shirt that read:

PAYSAN
Et fier d'être
(Peasant and proud to be)

A local winegrower and president of the cooperative, Thoulouze was to be my guide that morning in the ancestral home of chatus. Thoulouze squeezed back into the Clio, tossing a handful of papers from the passenger seat into the rear and on the floor. I got in, and immediately as we left D104 and started climbing the Cévenole, we were in another world.

Thoulouze drove up winding roads and down into a valley and up again. There were vines, forests of chestnut trees, and more vines. But the most outstanding feature of the terrain was the way in which it was terraced. Miles of typically waist-high dry walls— made without cement from artfully stacked tan and gray stones— formed an endless ribbon that wrapped around every hillside and every contour of the landscape. This sort of terracing was used by southern European paysans for centuries as a means of leveling the landscape and protecting soils and crops from washing away. Many of the stone walls were partially buckled or pregnant-looking, or sprouted wildflowers and small trees in the spaces between the stones. Some of the walls held up terraces of orderly vine rows and olive groves. Others suffered from neglect: between broken walls were jungles of bramble or spontaneous stands of pine.

"We are winegrowers and masons at the same time," Thoulouze said, pushing his foot into the accelerator as we banked around a hillside. He was forty-three, a fourth-generation winemaker from these hills, and, I noticed, he had the thick fingers of a stoneworker.

We stopped on a plateau from which we could survey a landscape that included some of Thoulouze's vines. It is an open, hilly countryside of small peaks and valleys of farmhouses and tractors. While the walls hold up the terraces, there are no fences or gates separating neighbors. In all, Thoulouze noted, he has thirty-seven acres of vineyards, a little more than an acre of which is young chatus, and more than four miles of wall to maintain.

The hills of the Cévenole are not radically steep. Still, the terraces were built primarily in the sixteenth and seventeenth centuries to keep the fragile soils intact. Thoulouze walked over to a plot of vines at the side of the road in which the soil had been recently turned. He grabbed a handful of dirt and feathered it between his fingers.

The stuff was unlike any soil I'd seen in a vineyard—light, peaty, powdery. The subsoil, he explained, is sandstone—decomposing granite in various stages—from which the terraces and farmhouses were built. Without the terraces, Thoulouze said, the vineyards would have disappeared long ago.

Thoulouze then explained how the walls were built using primitive techniques that are still used to maintain the terraces. "They turned the soil, and used the stones from the subsoil. You have to be quick, you have to cut the stone—*tack tack* . . . ," he said, illustrating the technique with an imaginary hammer and chisel. "Then you place it on the wall and you put some dirt there and continue back to the soil."

Here in the vin de pays, non-appellation wine country of France, the recompense is not great. Working on circuitous terraces and maintaining them adds about a third to winegrowers' costs, Thoulouze said. In a country where workers punch out after thirty-five hours a week and receive five weeks of vacation, Thoulouze said that he, like most winegrowers, works two French work weeks in one in warm months and seldom takes a holiday. "But I prefer to work in my vines instead of taking the metro to work everyday in Paris or Lyon," he said. The greatest challenge for us is passing our traditions along to the future generations."

With every generation, young people were selling out and moving to French cities or to London. Not everyone born here was willing to take up the banner of proud paysans. "The problem in France is we have fewer and fewer workers. But a France without *paysans* would be a disaster," Thoulouze said on the way back to the car, and for emphasis he repeated *désastre*. "If tomorrow there are no *paysans*, there will be no more savoir faire. And there will be no more good sense."

Back in his car, we continued on—spiraling through hills and farm hamlets. Then I was struck by something so familiar and, at the same time, shockingly out of place: a small grouping of modern houses. Three of them made their own small patch of suburbia. The places had fine views of the countryside, but with their green squares of lawn and chain link fencing were resisting becoming part of their surroundings. Unlike the sandstone farmhouses, these homes were built in cinderblock and painted in bright Provencal colors of terra cotta and ochre. The inhabitants were perhaps city people and these were presumably secondary residences.

"Vacation homes?" I asked Thoulouze.

He nodded. "The real estate people come, they buy, they construct," he said. "And our history disappears little by little. The bulldozers come and destroy the walls. It makes you sick at heart. They come and destroy the work of the *paysans*. Five hundred years of history like that! Patrimony and sentimental value mean nothing to them."

Sentimental, I thought—the same word in French and English— how odd to hear a guy who looks like Thoulouze speak so unabashedly of sentimental value.

A road sign announced that we were entering the hamlet of Chateauneuf. An old man wearing a gray paysan's cap waved to Thoulouze, who pulled the car to the side of the road and cut the motor. We got out there in the middle of the road that divided a house from its garden and its acres of vines. The man was Charles Chabane, an eighty-four-year-old vintner who now leases out his five hectares of vines to a young grower nearby. Chabane's wife, Lucette, holding a small garden trowel and a box of seeds for peas, came over to join her husband.

Chabane, Thoulouze recounted, had been one of the original founders of the Rosières cooperative. And Chabane began reminiscing about winemaking here half a century ago. "We mixed all the varieties together," he said, "aramon ... syrah ... chatus ..." Chabane kept going on: "allicante ... gamay also. ..."

Suddenly a few yards away, rising up on the crest of hill, there appeared a man pedaling a bicycle. It was no ordinary-looking man or bicycle. Rather, the man could have been an alien clad in red spandex. His ensemble was topped by wraparound mirror glasses and a racing helmet that looked like a piece of sculpted wind. The color-coordinated shoes were clipped to tiny pedals the size of a coin and the man and machine fused into a whirl of red and black and chrome.

Thoulouze and Madame Chabane turned to see this sight. Monsieur Chabane reeled around a complete 360 degrees as he bent at the waist and stared as though a meteorite had just landed in his vines. The cyclist, for his part, ignored us, head pointed forward and down as he spun his pedals past us and out of sight. There was not—and this is rare in the French countryside—a breath of "bonjour" from anyone.

Monsieur Chabane then turned back to me with a lost look, as though he'd forgotten how I got there.

"Chatus . . . ," I said.

"It improved the wine . . . I still have one vine. Exactly one," he said, pointing across the road, up behind his house.

We said our *au revoirs* and shook hands all around. Thoulouze and I got back into the Clio and he repeated what I noticed was a ritual every time he restarted the car. He turned the ignition, the motor hesitated, and he appeared to be counting to himself, nodding his head in rhythm, "un, deux, trois," and then nothing. Then Thoulouze turned the key again, "un, deux," and the motor started up and we continued on to the hamlet of Vernon. We crossed another stand of chestnut trees, then a creek, and climbed up a road that was no wider than Thoulouze's Clio, with weeds intruding in the center. At one point, we stopped until a napping dog vacated his spot in the road.

Thoulouze brought the car to a stop on a perched vineyard below a sprawling, uninhabited farmhouse made from the same (*tack, tack*) stones that formed the walls all around us. This was the vineyard of ancestral chatus vines owned by Allamel's family and planted more than 120 year ago, and I approached it with something close to reverence. It was like no other vineyard I'd seen.

There were thousands of vines planted mostly in orderly rows and trained on wire between wood stakes. But the trunks and limbs of these vines resembled trees more than vines and had been allowed to grow in circular, contorted patterns. The bark was flaky, almost hairy. The vines looked to be simultaneously in action and arthritic—like souls trapped in wood.

Some were not part of the trained vine rows at all but stood at the foot of terraces as tall as a man. They rose over the stones and then turned parallel to the ground running a good ten feet and grabbing onto fence posts or guiding wires.

"Can you imagine all the things these vines have to tell?" Thoulouze said, breaking the silence. "All the stories they've heard between men."

Thoulouze found a vine with a still-uncut shoot and illustrated how the shoot would bear fruit one year and the next would have to be cut away. Each time as the vines were pruned they had to be cut at the fourth bud, as the first three were sterile. He picked up a cutting from the ground that was pliable, pulled a knife from his pocket, and demonstrated the traditional technique of attaching vines to guide wires using a vine cutting. He seemed to have been able to do the whole procedure in a second. "You put a young person in here to cut these vines, and they would be lost," he said.

Jacquez, which was introduced following the phylloxera outbreak of 1870, was banned as varietal in France in the 1930s (for what were called "foxy" flavors of the grapes). As a rootstock, it has all but disappeared, replaced by modern and more practical stocks—even in the young chatus.

We climbed in the car and Thoulouze started it—again making two attempts as the motor hesitated before summoning enough energy to turn over.

"Nowadays, to find out the weather you have to call the *meteo* [weather service]!" Thoulouze was saying. "People used to *smell* the coming rain. They would listen to the frogs." He said, "They knew that when the clouds go north it means rain, when the clouds go south it means good weather. And when you see a scorpion, it's going to rain three days later."

As the road leveled off back near the center of town and the road that connects Rosières to the rest of the world, we passed one particularly high stone dry wall of about twelve feet, with perfectly chiseled stones aligned at right angles.

"Look at that, it's . . . ," Thoulouze sighed as he made a hand gesture—a sort of perpendicular chop in the air to illustrate the flawless corner. "The people who built these walls were passionate about their work," Thoulouze went on. "It is . . . truly . . . architecture."

"Passionate," "sentimental" . . . some of the words Thoulouze had used stuck with me. For him, it seemed, wine represented something far greater than I'd once imagined it could. Wine was an order, a social structure that was diminished by each dry wall destroyed by neglect or the bulldozer. The old chatus vines were like those walls. They gave meaning and definition to a landscape that would otherwise tumble into anarchy. All of it—the walls, the vines, soil, the chatus—formed a bulwark against a world that at times seemed incomprehensible.

That evening—light and clear and lit by an orange glow—I returned to those hills of the Cévenole. This time I went with my wife to meet Christophe Reynouard.

In the world of chatus, there are not many players. The Cévenole cooperative is responsible for about three-quarters of the production of chatus wine. Three other nearby cooperatives sell some as well. And then there is Reynouard, with his tiny Domaine du Grangeon, the only independent winemaker in France—and perhaps the world—who makes chatus.

A fifth-generation winegrower on his grandfather's side (and further back on his grandmother's), Reynouard is a slight man with jet-black hair who looks a decade younger than his thirty-eight years. We met in his winery, which he constructed in what were the stables of his grandmother's farmhouse on a plateau above the hamlet of Balbiac—a bend in the road where there is a small collection of old sandstone houses surrounded by vineyards in all directions.

Reynouard fetched us glasses and we met two other visitors, a local winegrower named Jean and his friend, who, it seemed, had been drinking for some time that day. Jean is typical of the locals you meet in wineries in the French wine regions around sunset, the hour when spitting wine is no longer an option. He was sixtyish with a belly, a carbuncle of a nose, a permanent mischievous smirk, and a repertoire of wisecracks and off-color humor.

We tasted our way through steel tanks of Reynouard's whites, made principally from viognier. At one point when Reynouard was explaining some arcane aspect of French wine regulation, Jean boasted, "In my life I try to do only things that are forbidden."

Reynouard's interest in chatus goes back to the initial trials at the

Cévenole cooperative where he had been an intern after finishing his lycée studies. "I participated in the vinification and I found it exciting," he said. "It was a wine that was more tannic than cabernet sauvignon, but with a very high acidity like pinot noir. It pleases some people enormously and it displeases others enormously—there is no in between."

Reynouard explained that his initial experience with chatus prompted him in the early 1990s to plant several acres of it on his family's land, which had included exactly fifteen old chatus vines. After working for an older winemaker in Condrieu in the northern Rhône Valley from 1993 to 1997, Reynouard returned home to Balbiac to establish a winemaking operation independent of the cooperative.

Over the course of the next half-hour, we followed Reynouard down some stairs into a cellar where we tasted his syrah from wood barrels. So where, I asked, was the chatus? Reynouard led us back upstairs into a section of the winery where he kept his tractors and other farm equipment. There, off in a corner, were a couple of rows of new oak barrels.

I was shocked on two counts. Reynouard appeared to be a serious, conscientious winemaker who made several cuvées of whites, rosés, and reds. Among them all, his chatus could be called his prestige red—selling as it did for 10 euros a bottle. (Because local demand outstrips the small quantities, he limits sales to three bottles per year per family.) Why, I wondered, wasn't it in his cellar in an ideal damp, cool place? What was it doing up here next to the farm equipment in a room that might vary in temperature from near freezing in winter to a hundred degrees in the dog days of summer. And secondly, why was Reynouard laying down his chatus on all *new* wood? Wouldn't that, after all, dominate the wine?

Reynouard's answer to those questions was "non" and "non." Chatus, he said, was far too aromatic, tannic, and acidic to be dominated by wood, and at the same time it needed to oxidize and evolve to reach its potential. Because of its high acidity, it needed very little sulfites, yet used barrels require some sterilization with sulfur, which, he reasoned, would inhibit the evolution of this wine. Therefore, the new wood.

Reynouard then went off into the corner, mounted his stack of chatus barrels and came back with a pipette of his 2005 vintage.

To fully develop, he said, it needed to work—not be babied. He left it in the barrels—unfiltered on its lees—to shiver, sweat, and vibrate next to his tractor engines for two years before putting it in bottles. "That's my secret," he said. "It's a demanding grape. It's demanding in the cuve and it's demanding when it's being raised."

He siphoned samples into our outstretched glasses.

"My two favorite grapes are syrah and chatus," he said. "Syrah because you can't cheat it. You can plant it all over, but to have those aromas of violet and the typicity you have to have small yields."

"And chatus because it's demanding . . . Anybody can make merlot. You just pick the grapes, put them in the cuve, and go on vacation, but chatus requires work," he said." Also we are just learning about chatus. We are still learning, every year."

The smell was now familiar: the potent whiff of tanned fruit leather I'd breathed in the La Cévenole cooperative's bottle and which led me to Reynouard's door. "Nèfle," Reynouard said, using the same description that Allamel had given me that morning. *Nèfle* is the French word for medlar, a small, rustic fruit that's sort of a cross between a pear and hawthorne. Ironically, it is often described as having "winey" qualities. Like chatus, nèfle is an odd species—a tough, meaty fruit—that doesn't like to be pampered and is often left on straw to soften and ferment a bit before consumption.

I let the scents of nèfle drift up through my sinuses, and raised the glass and sipped and . . . and *nothing*! The wine was tasteless: all shapeless tannins and rude acidity. In a word: undrinkable. Puckering faces were made all around.

"The attack in the mouth is not there yet," Reynouard said. Then Reynouard went back with his pipette to his barrels for another sample, and came back with the 2004 vintage.

Once again, the big bouquet that filled my sinuses, and then the sip and . . . zero! This wine, like the previous sample we had tasted, apparently still hadn't had enough time to synthesize—to be whipped into shape in those garage barrels.

After I poured out the rest of what was in my glass down a floor drain, Reynouard said, "Now smell the glass." I held the empty glass to my nose: the explosion of aromas—the nèfle—was still there. "That," he said, "is chatus—right there."

We drove in our cars with our glasses to Reynouard's family house down the road in Balbiac from where his parents sold his wines along with garden vegetables, fruits, and eggs. There, Reynouard produced a bottle of his 1999 chatus and poured.

Again, the smell held out the promise of good things to come. I sipped, expecting nothing. But this time as the scents mingled somewhere in my midbrain, their corollary tastes rolled across my tongue. It was all there: the nèfle, the fruit leather, the tannins, the finesse, the chatus.

"Ça," said Jean, using my favorite French hyperbole. "C'est le petit Jesus en culottes de velours."

Little Jesus in velvet knickers indeed.

For Reynouard, it was something more—inseparable from the generations that came before him and worked these hills. "It is us," he said. "Gamay is Beaujolais," he went on. "Pinot noir is Burgundy, merlot and cabernet are Bordeaux, and chatus is . . . us."

"Good or bad, *c'est nous.*"

It was not a wine that would revolutionize the world. It would not soon be in wine auctions or sold in the chic restaurants of world capitals. But as I left the Cévenole the following morning, I was awed by the fact that something so good could exist on such a secret scale. Discovery in wine, it seemed, was still possible.

I had once lost faith in wine in cynical been-there-drunk-that Bordeaux, and I'd regained it on a road that led to hamlets like Balbiac that don't appear on the map.

"*Nous.*"

Where goes chatus goes France, I reasoned.

Where goes France goes wine.

And where goes wine, we all go.

14. A century-old chatus vine

Appendix

Château Soutard
33330 Saint-Émilion
+33 (0)5 57 24 72 23

François des Ligneris
Une Affaire de Familles
1, Rue de la Liberté
33330 Saint-Émilion
+33 (0)5 57 24 91 62
www.uadf.com

Cassini
Arnaud Daudier de Cassini
Lartigue
33330 Saint-Émilion
+33 (0)5 57 24 73 83
http://cassini.viticulteur.free.fr/

Jean-Bernard Siebert
67120 Wolxheim
+33 (0)3 88 38 43 92

Domaine Borrely-Martin
83340 Les Mayons
+33 (0)4 94 60 09 39

Château Pradeaux
676 Chemin des Pradeaux
83270 St-Cyr-sur-Mer
+33 (0)4 94 32 10 21

Domaine d'Alzipratu
20214 Zilia
+33 (0)4 95 62 75 47

Domaine Cazes
4 rue Francisco Ferrer
BP 61
66602 Rivesaltes
+33 (0)4 68 64 08 26
http://www.cazes-rivesaltes.com

Domaine Mas Amiel
66460 Maury
+33 (0)4 68 29 01 02

Cave de Caramany
66720 Caramany
+33 (0)4 68 84 51 80

Château Mossé
Sainte-Colombe-de-la-
Commanderie
BP 8, 66301 Thuir
+33 (0)4 68 53 08 89
www.chateau-mosse.com

Domaine Leon Barral
Lenthéric
34480 Cabrerolles
+33 (0)4 67 90 29 13

Mas de la Seranne
34150 Aniane
+33 (0)4 67 57 37 99
www.mas-seranne.com

Gilles Barge
8, Boulevard des Allées
69420 Ampuis
+33 (0)4 74 56 13 90

Jean-Michel Stephan
RN 86
69420 Tupin-Semons
+33 (0)4 74 56 62 66

Domaine d'Escausses
81150 Sainte-Croix
+33 (0)5 63 56 80 52

Robert and Bernard Plageoles
Domaine des Tres Cantous
81140 Cahuzac-sur-Vere
Domaine Roucou-Cantemerle
81140 Castelnau de Montmiral
+33 (0)5 63 33 90 40

David Duband
21220 Chevannes
+33 (0)3 80 61 41 16

Vignoble de la Coulée de Serrant
49170 Savennières
+33 (0)2 41 72 22 32

Cave Cooperative La Cevenole
07260 Rosières
+33 (0)4 75 39 90 88

Domaine du Grangeon
Balbiac Rosières
07260 Joyeuse
+33 (0)4 75 39 54 84

Recovering Our Ancestors'
Gardens
Indigenous Recipes and Guide
to Diet and Fitness
Devon Abbott Mihesuah

Dueling Chefs
A Vegetarian and a Meat Lover
Debate the Plate
Maggie Pleskac and
Sean Carmichael

A Taste of Heritage
Crow Indian Recipes and
Herbal Medicines
Alma Hogan Snell
Edited by Lisa Castle

The Banana
Empires, Trade Wars, and
Globalization
James Wiley

AVAILABLE IN BISON BOOKS
EDITIONS

The Food and Cooking of
Eastern Europe
Lesley Chamberlain
With a new introduction by
the author

The Food and Cooking of
Russia
Lesley Chamberlain
With a new introduction by
the author

The World on a Plate
A Tour through the History of
America's Ethnic Cuisine
Joel Denker

Jewish American Food Culture
Jonathan Deutsch and
Rachel D. Saks

The Recipe Reader
Narratives, Contexts, Traditions
Edited by Janet Floyd and
Laurel Forster

Masters of American Cookery
M. F. K. Fisher, James Beard,
Craig Claiborne, Julia Child
Betty Fussell
With a preface by the author

My Kitchen Wars
A Memoir
Betty Fussell
With a new introduction by
Laura Shapiro

Good Things
Jane Grigson

Jane Grigson's Fruit Book
Jane Grigson
With a new introduction by
Sara Dickerman

Jane Grigson's Vegetable Book
Jane Grigson
With a new introduction by
Amy Sherman

Dining with Marcel Proust
A Practical Guide to French
Cuisine of the Belle Epoque
Shirley King
Foreword by James Beard

Pampille's Table
Recipes and Writings from
the French Countryside from
Marthe Daudet's Les Bons Plats
de France
Translated and adapted by
Shirley King

Moveable Feasts
The History, Science, and Lore
of Food
Gregory McNamee

To order or obtain more information on these or other University of
Nebraska Press titles, visit www.nebraskapress.unl.edu.